Health Psychology:
Stress, Behaviour and Disease

ЛT

Series Editor: Professor Raymond Cochrane
School of Psychology
The University of Birmingham
Birmingham B15 2TT
United Kingdom

This series of books on contemporary psychological issues is aimed primarily at 'A' Level students and those beginning their undergraduate degree. All of these volumes are introductory in the sense that they assume no, or very little, previous acquaintance with the subject, while aiming to take the reader through to the end of his or her first course on the topic they cover. For this reason the series will also appeal to those who encounter psychology in the course of their professional work: nurses, social workers, police and probation officers, speech therapists and medical students. Written in a clear and jargon-free style, each book generally includes a full (and in some cases annotated) bibliography and points the way explicitly to further reading on the subject covered.

Psychology and Social Issues:
A Tutorial Text
Edited by Raymond Cochrane, *University of Birmingham* and Douglas Carroll, *Glasgow Polytechnic*

Families: A Context for Development
David White and Anne Woollett, *Polytechnic of East London*

The Psychology of Childhood
Peter Mitchell, *University College of Swansea*

Health Psychology: Stress, Behaviour and Disease
Douglas Carroll, *Glasgow Polytechnic*

Forthcoming titles:

Adult Psychological Problems: An Introduction
Edited by Lorna A. Champion, *Institute of Psychiatry, London* and Michael J. Power, *South East Thames Regional Health Authority, Kent*

On Being Old: The Psychology of Later Life
Graham Stokes, *Gulson Hospital, Coventry*

Food and Drink: The Psychology of Nutrition
David Booth, *University of Birmingham*

Health Psychology:
Stress, Behaviour and Disease

Douglas Carroll

 The Falmer Press

(A member of the Taylor & Francis Group)
London • Washington, DC

UK   The Falmer Press, 4 John Street, London WC1N 2ET
USA The Falmer Press, Taylor & Francis Inc., 1900 Frost Road, Suite 101,
Bristol, PA 19007

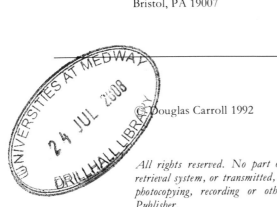

First published 1992. Reprinted 1995

A catalogue record for this book is available from the British Library

Library of Congress Cataloging-in-Publication Data are available on
request

ISBN 1 85000 841 8
ISBN 1 85000 842 6 (pbk)

Jacket design by Benedict Evans

Typeset in 10.5/11.5pt Garamond
by Graphicraft Typesetters Ltd., Hong Kong

*Printed in Great Britain by Burgess Science Press, Basingstoke on paper which has a
specified pH value on final paper manufacture of not less than 7.5 and is therefore
'acid free'.*

Contents

Acknowledgments   vi

Series Editor's Preface   vii

Chapter 1   Introduction: Stress, Behaviour, and Disease   1

Chapter 2   Type A Behaviour and Coronary Heart Disease   11

Chapter 3   Hypertension and Cardiovascular Reactions to Stress   22

Chapter 4   Cancer and the Immune System   33

Chapter 5   The Challenge of AIDS   43

Chapter 6   Stress Management: Reducing the Risk of Coronary
              Heart Disease   54

Chapter 7   Exercise, Fitness, and Health   65

Chapter 8   Taking One's Medicine: Following Therapeutic Advice   75

Chapter 9   Pain and Psychological Approaches to its Management   85

Chapter 10   Final Comments: Gender, Race, Social Class, and Health   98

Bibliography   107

Note on the Author   123

Index   124

Acknowledgments

My particular enthusiasms within health psychology owe much to research collaborations with Paul Bennett, Gwen Cross, John Hewitt, Rick Norris, Jane Sims, and Rick Turner. Discussions with a number of other colleagues over the years have also helped shape my views; those that spring most readily to mind are George Davey Smith, Derek Johnston, Kate Niven, the late Paul Obrist, Andrew Steptoe, and David White. I owe a particular debt of gratitude to Ray Cochrane for his encouragement and support throughout. Finally, Cathie Wright turned my indescribably messy handwritten drafts into a neat word-processed manuscript, furnished coffee and biscuits, and generally kept me cheerful.

Series Editor's Preface

Before the beginning of this century the principal threats to health in most human societies were the contagious diseases which are those diseases caused by an invasion of the body by specific infectious agents. An analysis of the leading causes of deaths in 1900 showed that such things as smallpox, influenza, diphtheria, pneumonia, polio, tuberculosis and scarlet fever figured very highly. It was possible at that time to regard diseases as basically biological phenomena which could be influenced by social conditions such as the provision of adequate sanitation, but which were in many respects beyond the control of the individual who might be afflicted with them. In the final decade of the twentieth century this is all changed. It is now well known that the leading causes of death, at least in western societies, are heart disease, other problems associated with the cardiovascular system and various forms of cancers. In addition there are new diseases such as AIDS, which, while they are not yet significant in terms of total mortality rates in most societies, are a large threat to public health looming on the horizon. Now it has become the received wisdom that a great deal of the morbidity in modern societies, and indeed a great deal of excess mortality, is influenced to a substantial degree by the behaviour of individuals and the life styles they adopt.

In a recent textbook which included a chapter on the effects of stress on health the following disorders were listed as being linked to stress: the common cold, peptic ulcers, asthma, headaches, menstrual discomfort, vaginal infections, genital herpes, skin disorders, rheumatoid arthritis, chronic back pain, diabetes, hernias, glaucoma, multiple sclerosis, hypertension, and about fifteen other disorders. Indeed it is now hard to find a major threat to public health that is not assumed to have a behavioural correlate.

Health psychology has a relatively short history, but the past decade has witnessed an explosion of interest in this topic. Much of this interest stems from the discovery, or some might say the invention, of the 'type A' personality. Friedman and Rosenman in 1974 divided people into two basic types: type A and type B. The type A personality is marked by competitive, aggressive and impatient behaviour, and, it was suggested, is more prone to coronary heart disease than is the relatively relaxed, patient, easy-going type B personality. As the following pages make clear, the relationship is probably not that straightforward, but nevertheless the idea that personality type and behavioural style are linked to physical pathology triggered off many similar investigations.

Of course, there had always been evidence of direct links between behaviour and health, such as in the case of cigarette smoking and lung cancer. But since the advent of the type A studies, investigators turned their attention to more subtle relationships between psychological characteristics and health. At the same time as the type A concept was being developed, a new technology for measuring life events was also coming on the scene, and there was a parallel development of interest in the phenomenon of social support and how that might help people to defend against stress-related illnesses. The coincidence of changing morbidity patterns and advances on several fronts in social psychology generated the new discipline of health psychology. It is the new developments in these areas that are the subject of Professor Carroll's book. A glance at the list of contents will show the range of topics and their substantial significance for the health of everyone in the 1990s.

As with the rest of this series, the book has been written with a specific audience in mind. It is designed to be accessible to the beginning psychology student but to take that student, or any other interested reader, to a depth sufficient to enable them to feel a sense of satisfaction in being able to come to grips with the major theoretical and empirical perspectives that are influential in contemporary psychology. Professor Carroll has, himself, a distinguished record of research in health psychology and his own research and writing has substantially influenced the development of this field in Britain.

Raymond Cochrane
Birmingham
November 1991

Chapter 1

Introduction: Stress, Behaviour, and Disease

Health psychology is a broad church, but one of fairly modern construction. According to Matarazzo (1980) health psychology encompasses the total sum of the contributions that the discipline of psychology, the science of human behaviour and experience, has to make to the matter of physical health and well-being. The areas of such contribution range from the aetiological to the therapeutic; health psychology is concerned with untangling the psychological factors that contribute to the onset and course of illness and disease, and also with the application of psychological knowledge and techniques to the prevention and amelioration of disease, and the promotion of health. In addition, it has a regard to people's experience and behaviour in medical settings. Finally, health psychology is concerned with mental health and psychological disorders, such as depression, but only to the extent that these impinge on physical health. For the most part, though, mental health is the proper focus of clinical psychology.

Although the official delineation of these sorts of activities as health psychology is relatively new, the idea that psychological factors can contribute to physical illness and that essentially psychological techniques might be pressed into the treatment of illness and the promotion of physical well-being is far from new. The great physicians of antiquity realized that what might be manifest as physical illness and physical symptoms can often be traced to psychological antecedents.

By way of illustration consider a case reported by Galen from the first century AD (cited by Mesulam and Perry, 1972). The patient was an agitated and much troubled woman, complaining of a variety of physical symptoms. Examination revealed no apparent organic cause for the woman's malaise. However, during the course of the clinical interview, a bystander happened to mention that he had seen a young dancer called Phylades performing at the theatre. Galen observed that at the mention of this name, the woman's pulse became rapid and irregular. At subsequent consultations, Galen dropped the names of a number of dancers but without effect. Only the name of Phylades produced such turmoil. Galen deduced that it was unrequited love for this dancer which was the source of the woman's emotional agitation, and this emotional distress that underlay her physical symptoms.

It is only really in the later part of this century that these early lessons started to take on renewed significance. The end of the nineteenth and the beginning of the twentieth centuries were periods of substantial medical advance. However, this progress was very much founded on the idea that disease was the product of specific pathogens: germs that invaded the body and disrupted some aspect of its functioning. The belief in specific and single pathogenic agents encouraged the search for specific antidotes. The discovery of effective antidotes, for example vaccines, in turn reinforced the germ model of disease and illness. This overall approach, coupled with changes in environmental infrastructure, such as the provision of clean water supplies and the introduction of efficient sewage systems, was enormously successful. Infectious diseases that had previously debilitated or killed substantial numbers of people were virtually eliminated.

Two consequences of this achievement were soon evident. First of all, people, at least those in western countries, were living longer. This century has witnessed a substantial increase in average life expectancy. Second, people were succumbing to different afflictions; cardiovascular disease and cancer supplanted the infectious diseases as the major causes of death. It was soon apparent that the medical model, which had previously served so well, was hopelessly inadequate in the face of these new challenges, for these were multiply determined disorders, the products of a variety of interacting factors. Most importantly for present purposes, some of these factors were psychological, i.e., they had to do with the way people conducted themselves, their life styles, the sort of social and psychological environments they inhabited, as much as they had to do with physically noxious agents. Accordingly, there was once more the need to appreciate that mind and body are intimately intertwined: not only that psychological factors can and do contribute to the onset and progress of disease, but also that health, in general, is a matter of the mind as well as the body. It is people who get ill and must be treated. To isolate disease and treatment as topics only for the attention of medicine and biology is to misunderstand the nature of most contemporary illness.

The insights of Galen and the other great physicians of the past, that, in matters of illness and health, people's feelings, behaviour and social environment are important, are ignored at our peril. They are certainly at no time more pertinent than now. In one sense, health psychology can be considered an attempt to consolidate and build on these early insights, although, in another sense, it is very much a response to contemporary concerns. However, health psychology should not be seen as an attempt to supplant the biological focus of twentieth-century medicine, replacing it with a psychological focus. Rather, its orientation is interactive; its manifesto derives from the presumption that both biological and psychological processes contribute to illness and disease, and that biology and psychology, not to mention sociology and anthropology, have important contributions to make to understanding, remedy, and prevention.

Psychological Stress

A key concept in health psychology, and one that dominates much of this text, is psychological stress. In spite of this pivotal position, though, it has proved surprisingly difficult to obtain agreement among researchers as to the precise meaning of psychological stress. However, given the extent to which the term is now part of everyday vocabulary and that most people have some common understanding of what it signifies, issues of exact definition need not detain us overmuch.

The American physiologist, Walter Cannon (1935) was among the first to use the term stress in a non-engineering context, and clearly regarded it as a disturbing force, something which upset the person's equilibrium, disrupted the usual balance. Cannon applied the term homeostasis when referring to this equilibrium or balance. From a perspective such as this, then, stress refers to those events or situations that challenge a person's psychological and/or physiological homeostasis. Stressful circumstances are those which do not permit easy accommodation. Because of their meaning and the nature of the information they contain, individuals have to mobilize extensive psychological and/or physiological resources to deal with them; they cannot be handled 'on automatic'. What sorts of circumstances, then, are stressful and pose a challenge to homeostasis? Lazarus and Cohen (1977) offered a helpful taxonomy. They suggested that there were three broad classes of stressors, varying in the magnitude of the challenge posed, varying also in their persistence, and, finally, varying in the number of people affected simultaneously.

The first class, Lazarus and Cohen called cataclysmic events. Included here are natural disasters, such as earthquakes and floods, and also manufactured disasters such as war. Cataclysmic events are powerful in their impact and pose an enormous challenge to individuals. It is hardly surprising to find that, as a consequence, they can have a substantial affect on health and well-being. However, two other characteristics of cataclysmic events may serve to mitigate the worst of such effects. They are often short-lived, and they usually affect whole communities, i.e., everybody is in the same boat. Thus, the stress effects are not necessarily protracted and the people involved can rally together, providing each other with mutual support and comfort. We shall see later that social support can act as an effective buffer against the impact of stress.

A second class of stressors is what Lazarus and Cohen called personal stressors, and others have called negative life events. These are such things as the death of a close relative, divorce, loss of job, etc. They, too, represent powerful challenges, and are also, thankfully, in most cases, relatively short-lived in their impact. However, unlike cataclysmic events, personal stressors happen to fewer people at any one time. While most of us will experience the death of a close relative, for example, the experience will be individual rather than collective in the sense that different people have to face the experience at different times. This can have important implications, for the personal nature of such stressors limits the possibilities for broad social support, and the benefits that brings. There is substantial evidence that negative life events are associated with physical illness. Both objective symptomatology and subjective ratings of illness closely follow clusters of person stressors (see, e.g., Rahe, 1975; Rahe, *et al.*, 1970). Finally, while the occurrence of negative life events is clearly important, the absence of positive life events may also affect health in a deleterious fashion. For example, in a study of 18-year-old Swedes, those who exhibited high blood pressure reported significantly fewer positive life events in the previous two years than those who were not hypertensive (Svensson and Theorell, 1983).

The third class of stressors are what Lazarus and Cohen identified as daily hassles. These might be regarded as background stressors. While individually they are not nearly as powerful as cataclysmic events or personal stressors, they are omnipresent. What they lack in terms of magnitude of challenge, they make up for in terms of frequency and persistence. Thus, daily hassles are chronic rather than acute stressors, and it is this chronicity which makes them serious. In addition, daily hassles, like personal life events, are suffered individually. Although such hassles are undoubtedly the lot of almost everyone, each individual harbours the illusion that he or she is the sole victim. 'Why me?' is a common evocation. This presumption of personal victimization again reduces the likelihood of social support with its potential to buffer the effects of stress.

One common source of daily hassles is the work environment. A large body of research now attests to the pervasiveness of work stress and its impact on health. A few examples will serve to illustrate the association between stress at work and poor health. In a recent study of occupational stress among university employees, Carroll and Cross (1990) administered a battery of questionnaires to 1,000 academic and academically-related staff in seven British universities. In all, completed questionnaires were returned by 662 individuals, almost half of whom (49 per cent) indicated that they found their jobs stressful either often or almost always. Most importantly in the present context, job stress was found to have consequences for self-reported physical well-being. For example, of those who reported the poorest physical health (had scores in the highest third on a questionnaire measuring physical symptomatology), 81 per cent reported experiencing job stress often or almost always, whereas of those reporting the best physical health (having scores in the lowest third of possible scores on physical symptomatology), only 28 per cent reported experiencing stress often or almost always. In addition, of the various possible sources of occupational stress, it would seem that increased and conflicting job demands were the most reliable predictors of physical symptomatology.

Until recently occupational stress researchers have largely ignored university employees, presumably on the assumption that such occupations are relatively stress-free. The study reported above suggests that this is a highly questionable assumption. Frequent stress was reported by a substantial number of the respondents, and frequency of stress experience was found to have implications for self-reported health. In contrast, nursing has always been acknowledged to be a stressful profession. Gray-Toft and Anderson (1981) have identified seven major sources of stress within nursing: dealing with death and dying, conflict with doctors, lack of support, inadequate preparation, conflict with other nurses, workload, and uncertainty over treatment.

In a recent study of nurses working in National Health Service and private hospitals in Britain, Tyler *et al.* (1991) confirmed that, irrespective of the sector in which they were employed, nurses reported high levels of job stress. There were, however, differences in the apparent source of these high stress levels between the two sectors. Whereas conflict with doctors and uncertainty over treatment were more commonly reported as sources of stress by nurses in the private sector, stress derived from high workloads was more frequently cited by National Health Service nurses. In general terms, then, it would appear that whereas the physical environment, i.e., sheer workload, is a greater source of stress in the National Health Service, social and psychological aspects of the work environment present more of a problem to private sector nurses. However, irrespective of sector, it would appear that stress takes its toll in terms of health and well-being. Nurses in both sectors registered worryingly high scores on a questionnaire measure of symptomatology, and there was a significant positive association between the overall level of stress experienced and reported levels of symptomatology.

Both of these examples have relied on questionnaire measures of health, with all the attendant drawbacks. For example, it could be that a generally negative orientation towards life underlies both reports of high levels of job stress and protestations of poor physical health. However, while general negativity may be a factor, it is unlikely to account fully for the relationship reported in studies of this sort. Occupational stress is not only associated with subjectively reported levels of ill-health and symptomatology, but is also a predictor of objectively diagnosed illness and disease. For example, Alfredsson *et al.* (1985) conducted an analysis of deaths from heart disease across all occupational groups in Sweden. Occupations were classified in terms of high and low demand, and also as high and low in terms of the control over the work environment they afforded employees. Deaths from heart disease were found to be far more common among groups of workers who had the least control over what they did at work and when they did it, and who, at the same time, were in occupations with the highest demands. Theorell *et al.* (1985) reported further evidence of an association between occupational demand and control on one hand and objective health indicators on the other. Young workers in a variety of occupations monitored their own blood pressures once every two hours during a typical working day. Systolic blood pressure elevations at work were greater among those who were in high-demand/low-control occupations (e.g., waiter, cook) than those in low-demand/high-control occupations.

All of these studies suggest that work can be a potent source of background stress, that it can impose on the individual conflicting and often excessive demands, and that it contributes substantially to the daily hassles that individuals encounter. In addition, as we have seen, work stress can have deleterious effects on individuals' sense of physical well-being and objective indices of health.

Appraisal, Vulnerability and Coping

So far I have been talking about stress as if it is an objective characteristic of the environment. It is not. Stress, like beauty, lies in the eye of the beholder.

The point is nowhere better illustrated that in the research and writings of Richard Lazarus and his colleagues. For us to experience an event or situation as stressful, according to Lazarus (1966), we have to perceive or appraise it as such. Other appraisals, i.e., non-threatening appraisals, would serve to diminish the disruptive impact of the event, short-circuit the stress. An experimental study reported by Lazarus *et al.* (1965) provides a neat illustration of the point. Subjects viewed a stressful film called *Woodshop*, which depicted a series of gruesome accidents at a sawmill, such as a worker severing a finger. One group of subjects was encouraged to adopt a denial appraisal, by informing them, prior to viewing the film, that the participants in it were actors, that the events were staged and that no one was really injured. A second group was encouraged to use an intellectualization appraisal, and study the film from the vantage of its likely impact as a vehicle for promoting safety at work. A third group viewed the film without prior instruction. Heart rate and skin conductance were monitored throughout to gauge the physiological impact of the film, and subjects were quizzed about how stressful they found it. Subjects who had received either denial or intellectualization instructions showed less physiological disruption during the film and reported that it was less stressful than subjects given no appraisal instructions.

Thus, particular appraisals can ameliorate the impact of a potentially stressful event. There is a lesson of general significance to be learnt from this demonstration; there are psychological mechanisms at our disposal which may serve to combat stress. The existence of such devices has been recognized for some time. Freud referred to them as defence mechanisms, although today they are generally called coping strategies, and, to an extent, they help us explain why, in the face of a potentially stressful situation, some people yield but others do not. Part of the explanation is that some individuals have a fuller repertoire of positive psychological coping strategies. However, this is far from a complete explanation. Most current models of stress and illness postulate that stress precipitates illness where there is an existing vulnerability, a diathesis as it is sometimes called.

It is possible to regard this vulnerability as operating at a number of levels. First of all, it can operate at a biological level. Some individuals may simply be predisposed to suffer disruption to specific biological systems in the face of stress. There is now substantial evidence, for example, that individuals vary markedly in the physiological reaction they show to stress. In Chapter 3 I shall present evidence which suggests that, at least as far as cardiac reactions are concerned, variability to an extent reflects genetic predisposition. For the moment, though, let me briefly illustrate the general proposition by taking another example: pepsinogen and its role in ulcers.

It is generally conceded that psychological stress contributes to the development of ulcers, but stress cannot by itself afford a full explanation. The suspected mechanism is that stress causes an increase in the secretion of pepsinogen. Pepsinogen is secreted by the stomach and converted into pepsin, an enzyme which digests protein. Together with hydrochloric acid, pepsin constitutes the main active agent in the stomach's digestive juices. What is clear is that there are wide variations among individuals in the amount of pepsinogen they characteristically secrete. The research of Mirsky (1958) demonstrated that these individual differences showed familial aggregation, i.e., high levels of pepsinogen secretion ran in families. Additionally, identical twin pairs are far more similar in terms of pepsinogen secretion levels than are non-identical twin pairs. Because of the identical genetic profiles of identical twins, results such as this are generally taken to indicate a pronounced genetic influence, in this case on pepsinogen secretion levels. A study reported by Weiner *et al.* (1957) indicated just how stress and biological predisposition can interact to produce disease. The subjects were new recruits to the US army. Prior to their basic training, which is generally conceded to be extremely stressful, gastrointestinal examinations were undertaken. On the basis of the results, two groups of soldiers were selected, a group of oversecretors of pepsinogen and a group of undersecretors. None of the selected soldiers had ulcers at this stage. Approximately four months later, at the end of basic training, the soldiers were re-examined. Fourteen per cent of the oversecretors had now developed ulcers, whereas none of the undersecretors had. Thus, stress itself is a necessary but insufficient condition for illness; diathesis, in this case in the form of biological predisposition, must also be present.

Vulnerability may also operate at a psychological level. People vary in the stock of coping strategies they can tap and in their habitual coping styles. One such coping style is type A behaviour, where diverse environmental demands are dealt with by time urgency, competitiveness, and hostility. In the next chapter I shall discuss type A behaviour and its role in coronary heart disease. For the moment, though, it is sufficient to record that while this coping style may be just what the boss wants, it would not appear to be what the heart needs. Other coping styles may be more positively indicated. For example, there is evidence that the perception that one is in control of potentially stressful events reduces their impact (see, e.g., Glass and Singer, 1972).

Lastly, individuals may be rendered vulnerable at a social level. I have already mentioned the fact that what might be broadly termed social support serves as a buffer countering the worst ravages of stress. Briefly, social support refers to the provision of comfort, caring, esteem, or help by other people or social groups. Those without such a facility, without a close relationship, or a supportive social network, would seem to be at particular risk as a result. A few selected examples will serve to illustrate the protective role fulfilled by social support. Other examples emerge from the main body of the text: for example, in the discussion in Chapter 8 on adherence to medical advice.

First of all, let us consider the example provided by a study of psychological, as opposed to physical, well-being. I concede that this is not, as I have defined it, the proper remit of health psychology, but it is a study which shows very clearly the power of social support. Brown and Harris (1978) interviewed a sample of around 400 women living in Camberwell, South London. Between 20 and 40 per cent of them revealed a serious psychological problem during the preceding year. In the vast majority of instances, the problem was depression, and for most of these it could be traced to a particular stressful event, such as a bereavement. However, there was also a large number of women who had experienced a similar stressful event, but who had not developed mental health problems as a result. What rendered some women more vulnerable than others to stressful events? The study seemed to implicate a number of factors, but the most potent of them was the absence of a close and supportive relationship. Thus, an intimate and confiding friendship was observed to serve a protective function, reducing these women's vulnerability to stress, decreasing the likelihood that stress would have serious deleterious effects on mental well-being.

If we move now to the area of physical health, there is a growing body of evidence that social support offers protective advantage there too. For example, in the area of coronary disease and coronary disease risk, Orth-gomer and Unden (1990), in a ten-year study of Swedish middle-aged men, found that low levels of social support, measured in terms of recreational social activity, predicted death from coronary heart disease. Likewise, Blumenthal *et al.* (1987) observed that low levels of social support were associated with increased coronary atherosclerosis, generally considered to be a forerunner of serious coronary incidents.

Another related illustration is provided by research on recovery from a major coronary event. For example, Fontana *et al.* (1989) studied a group of seventy-three patients who had recently been admitted to hospital following a myocardial infarction (heart attack) or had undergone coronary bypass surgery. The patients were followed up for up to twelve months after discharge from hospital and various measures of stress, social support, and cardiac symptomatology taken. Psychological stress was found to exacerbate cardiac symptomatology, while social support ameliorated the subsequent experience of stress and had the opposte effects to stress on cardiac symptomatology.

Finally, there is recent evidence that social support may influence the effects of acute laboratory stressors on the cardiovascular system. Kamarck *et al.* (1990) measured the cardiovascular reactions of female students to psychological stress in one of two conditions. Either students were exposed to the stressors alone, or they were allowed to be accompanied by a friend, who would remain present throughout the testing. Subjects in this condition showed smaller cardiovascular reactions to the stress than subjects tested alone. If social support, as this study suggests, reduces the cardiovascular impact of psychological stress, this may be one mechanism through which social support exerts its positive influence on coronary heart disease risk, mortality, and recovery.

In summary, how psychological stress affects us depends on our vulnerability and the resources we have at our disposal to combat stress. Vulnerability would appear to operate at a number of levels: biological, psychological, and social. Chapters 6 and 7 look at the extent to which vulnerability can be reduced, in one case by applying stress management techniques, in the other by physical fitness and exercise programmes.

Levels of Influence

In a parallel fashion, stress itself can be regarded as eliciting effects at a number of levels. As Steptoe (1984) indicated, there are at least three basic routes through which stress can contribute to ill-health. First of all, stress can disrupt physiological homeostasis, provoking substantial reactions in various biological systems. I have already alluded to this. In Chapters 3 and 4, I shall examine in more detail the effects of stress on the cardiovascular and immunological systems respectively and the implications of such effects for disease.

Stress can also exert an influence at a behavioural level. Certain behaviours, cigarette smoking, excessive alcohol consumption, particular dietary habits, low levels of physical activity and exercise, have all been identified as contributing negatively to physical health and as positive risk factors for a range of diseases. While such behaviours have complex determinants, it is more than possible that one determinant is psychological stress. There is evidence (see Steptoe, 1984) that the incidence of such unhealthy behaviours increases during periods of stress.

Finally, stress may influence subjective symptomatology and what is called illness behaviour. Individuals vary markedly in the extent to which they perceive, acknowledge and respond to the physical symptoms of disease and illness. At one end of the scale we have hypochondriasis, where individuals are pathologically obsessed by symptomatology and constantly behave as if seriously ill, and at the other end, instances of sudden death, where there was little or no previously acknowledged symptomatology or medical consultation. It is possible that psychological stress may be one factor prompting individuals to attend more to symptoms of illness and seek medical advice. House *et al.* (1979) present an example. Subjective complaints of skin rashes and upper respiratory difficulties, coughs and excessive sputum, in a group of industrial workers were compared with reports of stress at work. A positive relationship was recorded; those who reported most work stress, complained most of physical symptoms. Further, in this particular study, work stress was not reliably associated with actual medical evidence of dermatological or respiratory problems; the relationship held only for subjective complaints of such problems. In Chapter 9, I shall consider the example of illness behaviour in the context of chronic pain, where it would appear that behaviour historically contingent on the experience of pain becomes, to an extent, dislodged from that influence, and is sustained by other, largely external factors. Thus, treatment, it has been argued, can be directed specifically at pain behaviour.

Behaviour

From the preceding discussion on vulnerability and the influence of stress on behaviour, it should be evident that how we conduct ourselves has important consequences for our health and well-being. For example, psychological stress can increase the incidence of unhealthy behaviours such as cigarette smoking and excessive alcohol consumption. Here behaviour increases our exposure to chemical toxins. In addition, in the face of stress, we adopt characteristic behavioural strategies. Not all of these strategies offer effective protection. Indeed, certain of them may render us especially vulnerable. In the next chapter, as indicated, we shall examine the possible pathogenic influence of one such strategy, type A behaviour, and in Chapter 4, consideration will be given to the possibility that a particular behavioural style may make us prone to cancer.

As indicated, social support, the sense of comfort and esteem we gain from others, can act as a buffer, mitigating the effects of stress. Energetic behaviours, that is vigorous physical activity and exercise, have been accorded a similar role. In Chapter 7, I shall examine the possible protective function of such behaviours.

I indicated previously that behaviours, such as cigarette smoking and excessive alcohol consumption, which put us at risk of disease, have complex social and psychological determinants. Stress is merely one component. Sexual behaviour is also multiply determined, and since unprotected sexual inter-course is the major route of transmission of the human immunodeficiency virus (HIV), infection with which causes acquired immune deficiency syn-drome (AIDS), the need to understand these determinants is urgent. If the catastrophic spread of HIV and AIDS is to be checked, individuals have to be persuaded to alter their behaviour. As we shall see in Chapter 5, this is no easy matter.

Chapter 2

Type A Behaviour and Coronary Heart Disease

Disorders of the cardiovascular system, especially coronary heart disease (CHD) and essential hypertension, have been among the most well-researched topics in health psychology. Given their prevalence, this is hardly surprising. Let us for the moment consider CHD. In western countries CHD is the most common cause of adult mortality, accounting for up to half of all adult deaths. In addition, behavioural factors (most noticeably cigarette smoking, diet, and physical inactivity) have been implicated in its development. Along with hypertension, which itself may, as we shall see later, have a significant psychological basis, these constitute widely cited risk factors for CHD. However, behavioural influences such as smoking and diet are relatively indirect; behaviour acts as an intermediary between pathogenic substances (in cigarette smoke or perhaps in our diet) and the cardiovascular system. In addition, even in the best combination, these traditional risk factors account for less than half of the new cases of CHD.

Much more exciting from a health psychology perspective is the prospect that our behaviour may exert a more direct influence, and that such a direct influence may explain some of the unexplained incidences of CHD. Like much of what I shall be discussing in this text, this is far from a new idea. It has been advanced by a number of eminent physicians throughout this century and even earlier. However, it was the research of two American cardiologists, Friedman and Rosenman, begun in the 1950s, that has most kindled recent interest. They elaborated the concept of type A behaviour, proposing a direct link between it and CHD.

Before considering type A behaviour, its measurement, its link with CHD, and the possible mechanisms of that link, it might prove useful to say something about CHD.

The Heart and CHD

The heart is in essence a pump, constituted of muscular tissue. Its job in the scheme of things is to ensure that oxygen-enriched blood from the lungs reaches the tissues that require it, and that the spent blood is recycled to the lungs for reoxygenation. The heart fulfils this task in a pulsatile fashion, beating approximately once every second when demands are minimal, but picking up the rate when the body's requirements for energy, i.e., oxygen, increase. Complex neural and chemical regulation ensure that the heart usually meets our needs, and the internal organization of the heart with its chambers and valves permits the proper sequencing of events.

However, the heart too has constant need of oxygenated blood to enable it to perform its life-sustaining work. This it receives through the coronary arteries, which depend, like other arteries in our body, on their elasticity and relatively large diameter to provide blood in the quantities required. However, the coronary arteries can become narrowed by the formation of fatty deposits, called plaques. We often refer to this process as 'hardening of the arteries'; medically, it is called atherosclerosis. CHD is thought to result from coronary atherosclerosis. As the inner walls of the coronary arteries become thick and hard, and elasticity and effective diameter reduced, so blood flow is impaired and the muscle fibres of the heart become increasingly oxygen-deprived. If deprivation is sufficiently severe the heart may cease to function altogether, and a myocardial infarction (heart attack) will ensue, with possibly a fatal effect. With less extreme, but nonetheless substantial oxygen deprivation, the outcome may be experienced as chest pains, particularly when the heart has to work harder to meet increased bodily oxygen requirements, as a result of physical or emotional exertion. This condition is referred to as angina pectoris. These then are the two major disease end points: myocardial infarction and angina pectoris. Both are thought to be a consequence of atherosclerotic degeneration of the coronary arteries and the resultant impairment of the heart's blood and hence oxygen supply.

Type A Behaviour

Let us now return to the concept of type A behaviour. It is a complex concept, but at its core is the notion of a behaviour pattern characterized by a chronic struggle to achieve more and more in less and less time, against the background of opposing and obstructive forces. The defining characteristics of this struggle and hence of type A behaviour are a strong achievement orientation, impatience, hostility and feelings of being under great time pressure. Thus, as originally conceived, type A behaviour is not a trait, i.e., not an enduring component of our psychological make-up or personality, that we carry around like our hand luggage into every situation. Rather, it is a complex of observable behaviours displayed by individuals in certain provoking circumstances. So, to echo Harvey (1988), it is not that someone is a type A person, rather that they are showing type A behaviour, i.e., what the type A concept was constructed to capture was a person-environment interaction. The relative absence of type A behaviours is referred to as type B.

Measurement of Type A Behaviour

In practice type A behaviour has been assessed both by interview and by questionnaire. Let us briefly look at the various methods in turn.

Historically the earliest assessment method, the structured interview (SI), as currently employed (Rosenman, 1978), comprises twenty-five questions, which probe the typical responses of individuals to everyday stressors likely to elicit impatience, competitiveness, or hostility. Concern lies not only with an individual's answers to these questions, but also with the style of behaviour displayed during the interview. The interview is conducted in a provocative style to maximize the likelihood of eliciting type A behaviour. As indicated, while the individual's answers to the questions are important in arriving at a final assessment, they are less important in practice than speech characteristics (interruptions, rapid speech) and overt displays of hostility.

Following the interview individuals are placed into one of four categories: A1, showing the fully developed behaviour pattern; A2, where many type A features are present, but not the full pattern; X, an equal representation of type A and type B features; B, the absence of type A characteristics. The interview is typically audio-taped, and is co-rated. Inter-rater agreement is generally high, but is better for the extremes than for individuals in the middle categories.

The most commonly used questionnaire assessment is the Jenkins Activity Survey (JAS) developed by Jenkins *et al.* (1976) as a questionnaire equivalent of the SI. The present version of the JAS type A scale comprises twenty-one items, although earlier versions contained as many as fifty items. Typical examples of the items included are:

> How often do you find yourself doing more than one thing at a time, such as working while eating, reading while dressing, or figuring out problems while driving?
>
> > A. I do two things at once whenever practical
> > B. I do this only when I'm short of time
> > C. I rarely or never do more than one thing at a time
>
> How often do you actually 'put words in the person's mouth' in order to speed things up?
>
> > A. Frequently
> > B. Occasionally
> > C. Almost never.

The Bortner Rating Scale (BRS) (Bortner, 1969) consists of fourteen bi-polar pairs of descriptors (e.g., never late/casual about appointments; not competitive/very competitive). Each of the pairs is separated by a 1.5 inch line. Individuals are asked to mark where on the line they would lie between the two extremes. The type A score is computed as the sum of the lengths of line measured from the type B pole of each descriptor pair.

The Framingham Type A Scale (FTAS) is a ten-item self-report measure of type A behaviour derived from the analysis of a large number of items completed by subjects in the Framingham Heart Study (Haynes *et al.*, 1978) The questionnaire contains items relevant to hard driving and impatient behaviour, as well as work pressure either in the home or workplace. An example of an item is: Do you get upset when your have to wait for anything?

Although the various measures of type A behaviour purport to measure the same thing, agreement between them is substantially less than perfect. In the original study of the JAS, agreement between it and SI assessment was 72 per cent. However, subsequent studies have found lower levels of agreement. Agreement between the SI on the one hand and the FTAS and BRS on the other appears to be around 60 per cent. Comparisons among the three question-naire measures indicate variable but again generally modest levels of agreement.

Given the different structures of the assessment methods, particularly between interview and questionnaire methods, but also among the three questionnaires, it is perhaps hardly surprising that research reveals only modest levels of agreement. For example, uniquely available from the SI assessment are actual speech characteristics, and, as indicated, these substantially inform the classification of the individual. Matthews (1982) has attempted to characterize what the different procedures are actually capturing about people. Individuals defined as type A from the SI, she argues, are those whose 'predominant behavioral characteristic may be a general reactivity to psycho-logical events that are frustrating, difficult, and moderately competitive'. JAS-defined type As, on the other hand, are 'vigorous achievement strivers, who can be aggressive and competitive'. The FTAS characterization she draws is almost the opposite of this. FTAS type As, she argues, are those 'dissatisfied and uncomfortable with the competitive orientation and job pressures that their lives entail'. It is perhaps little wonder, then, that there is only marginal overlap between measures. For a fuller critique of the type A measurement, the reader is referred to Bennett and Carroll (1989).

The Link between CHD and Type A Behaviour

The apparent strength of early evidence linking Type A behaviour and CHD was reflected in the Consensus Report (Review Panel, 1981), where type A behaviour was accorded equivalent status to traditional risk factors such as high cholesterol and hypertension. Since then, though, there has been increas-ing controversy. Let us consider the evidence, then, both early and more recent. Research in three key areas will be reviewed: prospective studies of healthy populations; studies of populations at high risk for CHD; studies of atherosclerosis.

Prospective Studies in Healthy Populations

The Western Collaborative Group Study (WCGS) (see Rosenman *et al.*, 1975) is without doubt the seminal study. Type A behaviour was measured using the

SI in a population of 3,154 male, predominantly white, non-manual workers aged between 39 and 59. All were free of CHD at the outset. Subjects were followed up for a period of eight and a half years. Over this period, those men assessed as showing type A behaviour were found to have an increased incidence of CHD compared to their type B counterparts; impressively, even when other risk factors were controlled for statistically, type As still had over double the risk of type Bs. Type A behaviour was more strongly linked to angina than to myocardial infarction, with relative risks of 2.5 and 2.1 respectively.

WCGS subjects have now been followed for twenty-two years (Ragland and Brand, 1988); 214 men have died from CHD, of which 119 were type A and 95 type B. This is not nearly such an impressive difference. Indeed, it can be argued that this result offers a serious challenge to the notion of a type A-CHD link. However, mortality from CHD does not equate with the incidence of CHD, and in fact, the original analyses at eight and a half years reveals that while type A behaviour is reliably related to the incidence, it is not so clearly associated with mortality. One plausible explanation here is offered by Bennett and Carroll (1990); it concerns the potential for behavioural change following the onset of disease. Type As with CHD who survive have the scope for making behavioural changes that could possibly retard further disease progression. Such a facility is unavailable to type Bs.

A total of 2,750 WCGS subjects free of CHD after two years of the WCGS were subsequently assessed using the JAS (Jenkins *et al.*, 1979). After four years, 120 subjects who had developed CHD were were matched with a larger randomly selected group of those who had not. Subjects in the upper third of the distribution of JAS scores displayed a risk of CHD almost double that of those with scores in the lowest third. A European study (DeBacker *et al.*, 1983) offers supportive evidence of a link between JAS scores and CHD. However, two other recent prospective studies, one of European men (Appels *et al.*, 1984) and the other of Japanese men living in Hawaii (Cohen and Reed, 1985) failed to find a relationship.

A similarly mixed picture emerges from studies that have used other questionnaire measures of type A behaviour. The Framingham study, using the FTAS, yielded positive results. A cohort of 580 men and 700 women aged 45 to 64 on entry to the study were followed for eight years. Both women and men who evidenced type A behaviour as revealed by the questionnaire were found to be at increased risk of CHD. However, while the effect held for all women, for men it was only apparent for those in white-collar occupations. The relative risks for total CHD, myocardial infarction and angina were 2.1, 1.3, and 3.6 respectively in women and 2.9, 2.3 and 1.8 respectively in male non-manual workers. Evidence from research using the BRS, though, is far less positive. While data from the French-Belgian Collaborative Heart Disease Study (1982) revealed a degree of association, two British studies (Johnston *et al.*, 1987; Mann and Brennan, 1987) failed to find any relationship between BRS score and later development of CHD despite the large sample size in each case.

To sum up, then, prospective studies offer some support for the notion of type A behaviour as an independent predictor of CHD. The strength of the link would appear to depend on the population studied (it is more apparent for those working in white-collar occupations, i.e., environments that might be regarded as more likely to elicit type A behaviours) and the method of type A assessment used (questionnaire assessment, particularly the BRS, yields less impressive evidence of a link).

Studies of High Risk Individuals

By far the most influential recent study of this sort is the Multiple Risk Factor Intervention Trial (MRFIT) (Shekelle *et al.*, 1985a). The SI was administered to 3,110 men aged 35 to 57 years, who were in the top 10 per cent of risk distribution for CHD based on blood pressure, cigarette smoking, and serum cholesterol levels. Following assessment, subjects were allocated to either usual care or special counselling. Type A behaviour was not associated with risk of CHD in either group at an average of seven years' follow-up.

The results have been regarded as particularly damaging to the type A hypothesis. However, it can be argued that what they actually reveal is that for individuals who are already at very high risk for CHD as a result of other factors, type A confers little or no additional risk. That is not the same thing as demonstrating that in a healthy population type A behaviour is of no significance.

Much the same can be said of studies which examine patients after they have suffered a heart attack. While an early study (Jenkins *et al.*, 1976) did report a positive relationship between type A behaviour, as measured by the JAS, and subsequent myocardial re-infarction, more recent research has not found such a relationship (Dimsdale *et al.*, 1981; Case *et al.*, 1985; Shekelle *et al.*, 1985b). For example, Shekelle *et al.* (1985b) examined the predictors of recurrent myocardial infarction in the 2,314 participants in a trial examining the effectiveness of aspirin in reducing the risk of re-infarction. All subjects were assessed using the JAS on entry to the study and were followed up for a minimum of three years. Type A behaviour was observed not to relate to re-infarction. However, all such studies demonstrate is that type A behaviour is not a risk factor for subsequent infarction in patients who already have substantial CHD. This does not necessarily refute the case that type A behaviour is predictive of the development of CHD in the first place. After all, the results of the Multicenter Postinfarction Research Study Group (1983) indicated that serum cholesterol, hypertension, and smoking were not predictive of re-infarction after an initial heart attack. Thus, although these traditional risk factors for CHD are predictive of onset, they do not seem to be predictive of recurrence, a picture very similar to that which appears to be emerging for type A. In short, the data from the high risk studies do not quite pose the threat to the type A hypothesis that a superficial analysis suggests. Rather, they indicate that whatever behavioural factors might be involved following disease onset, they are probably not the same as those which contribute to initial onset.

It might be argued that studies which look at the impact of changing type A behaviour in high risk individuals are of relevance here. So far only one such study has been conducted which adopted re-infarction as an outcome measure. For organizational reasons, I shall discuss this later in the book, in the general context of stress management approaches to cardiovascular disease (see Chapter 6).

Atherosclerosis Studies

One apparently simple procedure for testing the impact of type A behaviour on CHD is to examine the association between type A behaviour and the extent of atherosclerosis revealed during routine scanning by means of angiography. The reader will recall that athterosclerotic degeneration of the coronary arteries is considered to underlie much CHD.

In a series of studies using the SI, researchers at Duke University in North Carolina (Blumenthal *et al.*, 1978, 1987; Williams *et al.*, 1980) reported that the extent of type A behaviour correlated positively with the severity of atherosclerosis. Other, independent, studies have replicated these findings (Krantz *et al.*, 1979; Seeman and Syme, 1987; Frank *et al.*, 1978).

However, a number of other studies, also using the SI, have failed to find a relationship (Dimsdale *et al.*, 1979; Krantz *et al.*, 1981; Scherwitz *et al.*, 1983). These angiography studies are not without problems. First, in many there is an over-representation of individuals assessed as showing type A behaviour. This reduces the likelihood of detecting differences. Second, many have managed to examine only fairly modest samples. It is worth noting there that those studies which report an association between type A behaviour and atherosclerosis tend to have, on average, larger samples and a smaller percentage of type A subjects.

One substantial study, reported recently by Williams *et al.* (1988), undoubtedly provides the strongest evidence of a link. Nearly 2,300 subjects were studied. Type A behaviour was found to be reliably related to the degree of atherosclerosis, after other possible confounding factors, such as smoking, hypertension, and high serum cholesterol, were controlled for. However, the relationship held only for younger patients, those aged 45 or younger. Thus, as well as sample size and type A composition, we have perhaps to include age as a possible reason for the lack of agreement among previous studies. Studies which have used questionnaire methods of assessment have generally not found an association between type A behaviour and atherosclerosis.

Component Analysis

As indicated, type A behaviour is hardly unidimensional. Rather it encompasses a variety of behavioural orientations elicited by the appropriately challenging circumstances. Accordingly, it is of interest to examine which of the components of type A behaviour are most pathogenic. Such study might also help reconcile some of the inconsistencies in results, particularly those that seem to arise from the different assessment methods.

Two component analyses of the WCGS data have indicated anger and hostility as the main pathogenic element (Matthews *et al.*, 1977; Chesney, *et al.*, 1988). Interestingly, component analysis of the MRFIT study also revealed an association between CHD and measures of hostility. In addition, subsequent analysis of speech characteristics during the SIs demonstrated that increased CHD risk was associated with increased voice emphasis and shorter latency of answering questions (Scherwitz *et al.*, 1987). This all fits well with the outcome of studies which have specifically examined hostility in relationship to CHD. For example, Barefoot *et al.* (1983) tracked 255 physicians for twenty-five years following graduation and found a relationship between questionnaire hostility scores and subsequent CHD development. The CHD incidence for those scoring in the top half was nearly five times greater than bottom half scorers. In a subsequent study of lawyers, Barefoot *et al.* (1987) again found that those with the highest hostility scores had the highest CHD risk.

However, it should be conceded that not all studies which have attempted to relate hostility to CHD have yielded positive results. Nevertheless, sufficient have to suggest that this might be a major factor in the type A-CHD relationship. It would be oversimplistic, though, to propose that hostility is the only factor. After all, the Chesney *et al.* (1988) study, mentioned above, also indicated other components of the type A complex, such as fast speaking rate and competitiveness. It is the role of features such as these, as well as hostility, that probably explains why SI assessment has proved more predictive of CHD than some of the questionnaire methods.

Type A component analyses have also been undertaken in some of the atherosclerosis studies. Again, it is hostility which appears to emerge as the most consistent predictor (Dembroski *et al.*, 1985; MacDougall *et al.*, 1985). Further, while little evidence exists as yet, what there is suggests that hostility measured by more specific questionnaire is related to the degree of atherosclerosis, and, indeed, may be more strongly related than measures of global type A (Williams *et al.*, 1980).

Overview

If one presumes a hierarchy of the methodological strength of the various approaches to examining the relationship between type A behaviour and CHD, prospective studies that follow up healthy subjects at baseline appear the strongest. Evidence from angiographic and 'high risk' epidemiological studies adds to the picture, but should be accorded less weight. After all, these latter methods have frequently failed to find consistent relationships between other traditional risk factors such as smoking, serum cholesterol and blood pressure and CHD. With these reservations in mind, the prevailing evidence suggests some link between type A behaviour, as measured by the SI, and the development of CHD. Support emerges from the prospective study of healthy subjects and also from angiographic studies of atherosclerosis. This probably reflects the fact that SI measure of type A specifically includes assessments of hostility in determining the A type assessment. In addition, the ability to detect aggressive speech characteristics may also be crucial.

The original epidemiological evidence (Rosenman *et al.*, 1975) was based on a group of predominantly non-manual workers, and it may be that populations such as this may encounter more situations likely to provoke type A behaviours, have more control over their working environment, and more opportunities to seek challenging stimuli (Byrne, 1981). Accordingly, type A behaviour, measured at a point in time, may have more circumstantial relevance to non-manual populations. Support for this argument can be derived from the Framingham study where type A non-manual men and women in work had the highest levels of risk. This again reinforces the contention that type A behaviour should not be considered a stable undifferentiated response to all stimuli. Type A behaviour is elicited by environmental challenges and type As may in turn seek and elicit such challenge. Type A behaviour then, as I indicated at the outset, should be regarded as a dynamic person-environment transaction and not as a static trait. Finally, it is important to grasp that within the complex of type A behaviours, some may be more pathogenic than others; hostility has been shown to have a close relationship with the development of CHD.

How Might Type A Behaviour Contribute to CHD?

The precise mechanisms by which type A behaviour might make an independent contribution to CHD remain unclear. One possibility arises from the research of Manuck and his colleagues (Manuck *et al.*, 1983, 1989). The experimental subjects were monkeys fed on atherosclerosis-inducing (i.e., high cholesterol) diets. These animals then had their heart rates measured at rest and during the psychological stress of threatened capture with a large glove. Those monkeys who reacted highly, i.e., showed large heart rate elevations, to the stress were subsequently found to display greater coronary atherosclerosis than monkeys who showed relatively lower reactions to stress. These results raise the possibility that people who display type A behaviour may show larger cardiovascular reactions to the stresses and challenges of life than those who generally show type B behaviour, and that this greater reactivity contributes to increased atherosclerosis and consequently to CHD.

A substantial number of studies have now been undertaken to examine the relationship between behavioural style, i.e., whether people emerge as type A or B on interview or questionnaire, on one hand, and cardiovascular reactions to stress on the other. Few endeavours can have produced such contradictory findings. A number of researchers have reviewed these studies in detail and the reader is referred to these for a more comprehensive account than that offered below (Holmes, 1983; Houston, 1983; Krantz and Manuck, 1984; Myrtek and Greenlee, 1984). Given the variety of stressors employed and the different methods of assessing type A that have been used, it is perhaps hardly surprising that these studies have yielded different outcomes. However, taken as a whole, they cannot be considered as offering consistent support for the hypothesis that individuals judged as type A or B display differential cardiovascular reactivity to stress. For example, in Holmes' (1983) review, only six out of twenty-four studies revealed a reliable difference in heart rate, only four out of eighteen revealed differences in diastolic blood pressure, whereas only just over half (thirteen out of twenty) reported differences for systolic blood pressure. Moreover, even where differences were statistically reliable they were generally small in terms of absolute magnitude and accordingly unlikely to account for differential pathology.

An alternative hypothesis arises from the work of Byrne. Perhaps one of the difficulties with much of the research on cardiovascular reactivity and type A behaviour is that it very much treats type A behaviour as a trait, as a stable characteristic of individuals which even dictates the way their biology reacts to stress. Byrne's research reminds us of the original conception of type A behaviour, which, as I have indicated, is that of a person-environment interaction. What Byrne (1981) found was that individuals characterized as high in type A behaviour experienced significantly more stressful life events than those scoring low in type A, i.e., type Bs. Thus perhaps we should talk more about type A environments than type A individuals. However, individuals are not passive with regard to their environments, but active, manipulative agents. Thus, it is possible that those characterized by the type A behaviour pattern have organized their life styles in such a way as to increase the probability of encountering stressful events. This idea is certainly consistent with the epidemiological data reviewed earlier, and can accommodate the notion that stress is an important mediating factor. It is not that those assessed as type A react more to individual stressors, it is simply that they experience more stress and challenge, and it is the frequency of stress contact which may be the paramount factor in pathology. Certainly, there is evidence that the incidence of both stressful life events and stress at work contribute to CHD (see, e.g., Byrne, 1981; Alfredsson *et al.*, 1985).

Concluding Remarks

It would be all too easy for the reader to deduce from this treatment that CHD is a particular menace for those in what are conventionally considered as high pressure, and also generally high status, occupations, where the conditions and behavioural expectations are most conducive to type A behaviour. This would be wrong. CHD is still most commonly suffered by those in low status occupations. For example in a study by Marmot *et al.* (1984) of British civil servants conducted over a ten-year period, mortality (including CHD mortality) was three times greater in the lowest employment grades than in the highest grades. In addition, the greatest part of the difference in CHD mortality rates could not be explained by smoking, cholesterol levels or reported physical inactivity. Accordingly, traditional risk factors and type A behaviour considered together still leave a substantial explanatory gap. This is a matter I shall return to later. For the moment, though, it is worth making the point that while the influence of type A behaviour on CHD may be mediated through exposure to stress, type A behaviour would seem to increase contact with only certain classes of stressor, those that characterize essentially middle-class occupations and life styles. Those that beset individuals in lower social and occupational positions do not seem to be described by the type A concept, but are almost certainly potent contributors to the high incidence of CHD in such groups.

Chapter 3

Hypertension and Cardiovascular Reactions to Stress

While individuals exhibiting type A behaviour may not be reliably characterized by particularly large cardiovascular reactions to psychological stress,
excessive reactivity may still play an important part in cardiovascular pathology.
Specifically, as we shall see, the evidence seems to suggest that the manner of
an individual's cardiovascular reaction to stress may be of significance for the
development of hypertension. Since hypertension is a potent risk factor for
CHD, it may be in this way that relatively pronounced reactivity to stress
makes its contribution.

First of all, though, let us describe what we mean by hypertension, or to
give it its full diagnostic title, essential hypertension. Essential hypertension is
high blood pressure where there is no detectable medical or organic cause. The
vast majority of cases of high blood pressure are of this sort.

Blood pressure is a function of the volume of blood ejected by the heart
into the arterial circulatory system and the resistance offered by that system to
the passage of blood. When the heart is in its active or systolic phase, pressure
will be at a maximum as the ventricle chambers contract and forcibly eject
blood into the arteries. On the other hand, pressure will be at a minimum
during the heart's passive or diastolic phase. Accordingly, blood pressure is
described by two numbers; the highest is the pressure during the heart's
systolic phase, i.e., systolic pressure, while the lower figure signifies pressure
during the diastolic phase, i.e., diastolic pressure. In both cases, pressure is
measured in millimetres of mercury (mm Hg). In essential hypertension, both
pressures are excessively high. While definitions of what is 'high' vary slightly,
pressures above 150/90 mm Hg would be generally considered excessive. The
average blood pressure of young adults sitting quietly is approximately 125/75
mm Hg.

Essential hypertension is a substantial problem. It is estimated that as
many as 15 per cent of the adult populations of western countries exhibit high
blood pressure; world-wide estimates fluctuate around 10 per cent. Concern
with essential hypertension largely reflects its association with CHD and
stroke. The results of various studies testify that as blood pressure increases so
life expectancy decreases. At the outset of the Framingham study in 1949 (see
previous chapter) some 5,000 of the citizens of that small community in the

USA had their blood pressures recorded; about 20 per cent of them were revealed to have pressures in the hypertensive range. Kannel (1977) reviewed their subsequent medical progress and found that individuals with high blood pressure at outset were three times more likely to have suffered from myocardial infarctions and eight times more likely to have suffered strokes than those with blood pressures in the normal range.

While it is likely that a number of factors contribute to the development of essential hypertension, there is growing evidence that the way in which the cardiovascular system reacts to psychological stress may have an important role.

Autoregulation Theory

Drawing on the earlier ideas of Guyton and his associates (e.g., Guyton *et al.*, 1970), Paul Obrist (1976, 1981) outlined a possible mechanism whereby enhanced cardiac reactions to psychological stress could contribute to the development of high pressure. He suggested that some sorts of psychological stressor, those that demand active attention and vigilance, i.e., what he called active coping, but little in the way of physical demand, provoke in some individuals reactions of the heart that are unjustified in terms of concurrent levels of energy expenditure, i.e., sizeable increases in cardiac activity occur, but in the context of only marginal increases in energy expenditure. This pattern of reaction is in marked contrast to the individual's reaction to physical exercise, where the size of the increase in cardiac activity closely mirrors the increase in the physical demand of the exercise and energy expenditure of the individual. Thus, in some individuals psychological stress elicits what has been termed 'additional' cardiac activity, i.e., increases in cardiac activity over and above what would be expected on the basis of the physical energy demands of the particular psychological stress. This, according to Obrist, results in over-perfusion, particularly of skeletal muscle tissue. Blood is pumped to these muscles to an extent that is surplus to the muscles' requirements for energy, i.e., oxygen. This in turn precipitates autoregulation, i.e., adjustments to the circulation in order to compensate for the overperfusion. These auto-regulatory adjustments take the form of increases in arterial resistance.

The sequence outlined above, it is argued, determines that a sustained blood pressure increase occurs in the face of even the most transient psychological stressor. Blood pressure rises initially as a result of increased cardiac activity, and that elevation in blood pressure is then maintained, even when the cardiac increase subsides, by the autoregulatory increase in resistance. This theory further presumes that the repeated exposures to acute psychological stress in individuals who are highly responsive to it, and the relatively sustained blood pressure elevations that this provokes, over time lead to a resetting of an individual's blood pressure at a new and higher level.

Evolutionary Context of Cardiac Reactions to Stress

In many animals, including humans, imminent danger provokes marked cardiovascular activation, the purpose of which, it would seem, is to prime the animal for rigorous activity: what the American physiologist Walter Cannon (1935) called 'flight' or 'fight'. Clearly, at one time this preparation was of some significance for survival. However, the usual hazards or stresses that face those living in highly developed, technical societies are different from those that confront other animals and confronted prehistoric humans. Contemporary stresses are largely symbolic. They rarely involve immediate physical threats and hardly ever require vigorous action and high levels of energy expenditure. Nevertheless, it would appear that, for some individuals at any rate, these contemporary, more psychological stresses have the capacity to elicit vestiges of the 'flight' or 'fight' mobilization of the cardiovascular system. The result is, of course, an increase in cardiac activity that is 'additional' to requirements.

'Additional' Cardiac Activity

The first studies to provide sound evidence that periods of psychological stress were associated with greater cardiac activity than would be expected on the basis of an individual's concurrent levels of energy expenditure were conducted in Scandinavia. Blix *et al.* (1974) recorded heart rate, as an index of cardiac activity, and oxygen consumption, as an index of energy expenditure, in seven helicopter pilots and two transport aircraft pilots during flight manoeuvres, including take-off and landing. Measurements were also taken at ground level during rest and during maximal exertion on a treadmill. Plots of heart rate against oxygen consumption at rest and maximal exercise were used to compute what heart rate should be during flight maneouvres given the concurrent level of oxygen consumption. Actual in-flight heart rate was on average some 24 beats a minute higher than what heart rate should have been on the basis of the plots, i.e., there was some 24 beats per minute of 'additional' heart rate during flight manoeuvres.

In a subsequent study, Stromme *et al.* (1978) measured heart rate and oxygen consumption in thirteen parachute trainees at the Norwegian Army Parachute Training School just before and after jumps from the training tower. Heart rate and oxygen consumption were also measured at rest and during three increasingly demanding bouts of exercise on an exercise bicycle. The linear relationship between heart rate and oxygen consumption during the exercise phase of the study was then determined for each subject and used in conjunction with oxygen consumption measured before and after the jumps to obtain predicted heart rate values before and after the jumps. Comparison with the heart rate actually registered at these times again revealed marked discrepancies; on average actual heart rate was 40 and 60 beats per minute above the predicted values before and after the jumps respectively. As before, then, there was substantial 'additional' heart rate.

A series of more recent studies undertaken by the author and colleagues at the University of Birmingham have produced further confirmation. For example, Turner and Carroll (1985a) recorded heart rate and oxygen consumption during a video game and a challenging mental arithmetic task. This latter task consisted of addition and subtraction problems involving two-digit and three-digit numbers. Subjects were presented aurally with a problem and two seconds later with an answer; half of the given answers were correct, and half were incorrect. They were permitted just one second to indicate whether the given answer was correct or not, by raising the index finger of their right hand if correct and the index finger of their left hand if incorrect. Monetary incentives were used throughout to ensure interest. The video game was of the 'space invaders' type. On completion of these two tasks subjects exercised on a bicycle ergometer. Following a period of simply resting on the bicycle, they undertook four bouts of increasingly demanding exercise.

Heart rate and oxygen consumption values during the exercise phase of the study were employed, following the lead of Stromme *et al.* to obtain a regression line of heart rate on oxygen consumption for each subject. Examples of these lines for four of the subjects are shown in Figure 3.1. Also shown are data points for the video game and mental arithmetic. These particular examples were chosen to illustrate the range of profiles evident during psychological stress. The linear regression equations calculated for each subject were then used in conjunction with actual oxygen consumption values during the video game and mental arithmetic to predict heart rate values during the two tasks. These predicted values were, as would be expected from the plots above, considerably less than the heart rates actually recorded for subjects. The average 'additional' heart rate, the difference between predicted and actual, was 9 and 13 beats per minute for the video game and mental arithmetic respectively. However, these average values conceal enormous individual variation; for the video game the difference between actual and predicted heart rates ranged from −4 to +43 beats per minute, and for mental arithmetic from −4 to +35 beats per minute.

Subsequent research both by the Birmingham team (see Carroll *et al.*, 1990, 1991) and by researchers at the University of North Carolina (Sherwood *et al.*, 1986) has established that what is true of heart rate in such circumstances is also true of cardiac output, i.e., some individuals when faced with psychological stress show evidence of substantial 'additional' cardiac output. Overall, cardiac output is a function not only of heart rate but also of stroke volume, i.e., the volume of blood ejected from the heart on each beat. It is, in fact, excessive cardiac output that is the key factor in Obrist's theory. Thus the finding that it is not only heart rate but also cardiac output that can exceed expectations is an important one.

If such 'additional' cardiac activity constitutes a risk factor for the development of essential hypertension, one would expect a number of things to be the case: (i) cardiac reactions to stress would show a high degree of consistency across time and similar stress situations; (ii) since essential hypertension tends to run in families there should be a high degree of family resemblance with regard to cardiac reactivity; (iii) individuals known to be at risk for developing essential hypertension, by virtue of their parents having high blood pressure or because, as young people, they have relatively high, although sub-hypertensive, blood pressure levels, should show more excessive cardiac reactions to stress than those not at risk. Let us consider these in turn.

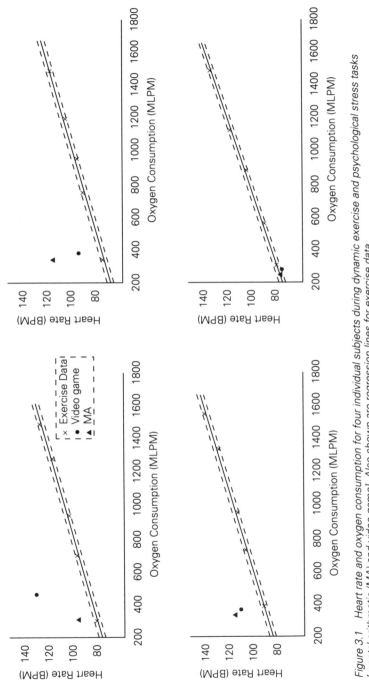

Figure 3.1 Heart rate and oxygen consumption for four individual subjects during dynamic exercise and psychological stress tasks (mental arithmetic (MA) and video game). Also shown are regression lines for exercise data.

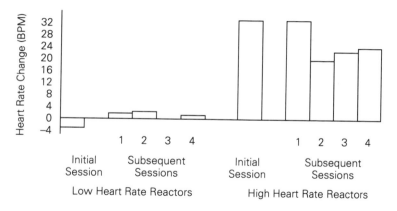

Figure 3.2   Average heart rate reactivity of high and low reactors

First of all, though, it is worth noting that established hypertension is not always associated with increased cardiac activity. However, we would not necessarily expect that to be the case. Once established, structural changes take place in the cardiovascular system of the hypertensive that maintain the condition. The issue is, though, how did the condition develop, and it is here that a role is postulated for excessive cardiac reactions to stress.

Temporal and Situation Consistency of Cardiac Reactions to Stress

Individual differences in cardiac reactions to the same stressor seem to be remarkably consistent across time, i.e., those who respond highly on one occasion do so on subsequent occasions. For example, Carroll *et al.* (1984) examined the heart rate reactions of twenty-three young healthy male students to playing a video game. The three most and three least reactive subjects were selected for further study. These six subjects returned to the laboratory a fortnight later and completed four more sessions with the video game; these sessions were scheduled on consecutive days. The average heart rate reactions of these three high and three low reactors are presented in Figure 3.2, inspection of which indicates a striking consistency of reaction over time. Although the high reactors showed some attenuation of reaction across sessions, by the final session their average heart rate reactivity was still around 24 beats per minute. The reactions of the low reactors remained minimal throughout. Although no one has examined consistency across a really protracted time scale, other evidence, using time scales longer than that reported above, also indicates substantial stability of reaction. For example, Turner *et al.* (1986) tested subjects' reactions to a video game on two occasions, with an average interval between occasions of twenty months. Heart rate reactions on the two occasions were exceptionally consistent.

Stability of reaction to different psychological stress tasks and, particularly, consistency between laboratory stress tasks and real-life situations, has proved somewhat more elusive. However, from the available research a number of conclusions can be drawn. Where studies have used laboratory stress tasks that are relatively similar in the psychological demand they make of an individual, i.e., require active attention and vigilance, high levels of consistency have been noted. Similarly, correspondence between laboratory and 'real-life' heart rate reactions is substantially greater where studies have used techniques that permit continuous, as opposed to intermittent, recording of heart rate in 'real life', have attempted to take into account postural differences (subjects are generally seated in the laboratory, but upright in 'real life'), and have attempted to control for movement, given that 'real-life' recordings are frequently made when subjects are ambulatory. Studies which have attended to one or all of these variables have generally found reasonable correspondence between the laboratory and the field.

The following two studies are included as illustrations. Turner and Carroll (1985b) recorded the heart rate reactions of forty-two undergraduate students to the video game stress used in studies reported earlier. Subjects were also monitored over a continuous eight-hour period while they went about their daily business. In addition, during this time, they kept a detailed diary of their activities, noting time, what they were doing, and whether they were engaged in high or low physical and high or low mental activity. (It was salutory to find one of the subjects reporting the hour spent in a lecture I was giving as low physical and low mental activity.) Minute-by-minute heart rate records and diaries for the eight hours were scrutinized by someone 'blind' to the subjects' laboratory reactions. Attention focused on periods of low physical/low mental activity (aside from my lecture, this was invariably periods of 'just relaxing', 'watching TV', 'listening to the radio'), and periods of low physical/high mental activity. Given the population from which the present sample was drawn, it is hardly surprising that the vast majority of the latter were periods of study. Other examples were stressful telephone conversations, driving in traffic and, in the case of two subjects, playing commercial video games. Problems with physiological recordings in a few subjects and activity reporting in many more reduced the effective sample size to thirty-one. For each of these subjects, the average heart rate during periods of low physical/low mental activity was calculated and subtracted from the average heart rate during periods of low physical/high mental activity. The difference between the two was taken as an index of 'real-life' heart rate reactivity to stress. This was then compared with the reactions recorded in the laboratory to the video game. The two measures were reliably correlated. More recently, Johnston *et al.* (1990) recorded heart rate reactions in the laboratory to a number of different stress tasks. These they characterized as either 'active coping' tasks (a video game, mental arithmetic) or a passive coping task (the cold-pressor test which involves placing a hand in a bucket of ice-cold water and keeping it there for a brief, but seemingly endless, period of time). Heart rate was also recorded continuously from subjects over a 24-hour period. In addition, physical activity was also monitored during this period, by measuring muscle activity from subjects' thighs. The 24-hour heart record was then amended statistically to remove any heart rate variations arising from variations in physical activity. 'Real-life' heart reactivity was defined as (i) the difference between sleeping and waking heart rate and (ii) overall heart rate variability during the waking day. These were then compared with reactions to the laboratory stressors. A fair degree of consistency was found between both indices of 'real-life' reactivity and laboratory reactions, but only for the 'active coping' laboratory stressors; no association was found between 'real-life' reactivity and heart reactions to the cold-pressor test.

In sum then, there is evidence that individuals show laboratory cardiac reactions that are highly consistent over time, reasonably stable across different 'active coping' stressors, and, although some counter-evidence exists, seem to reflect the pattern of heart rate activity displayed in 'real life'.

Within-Family Resemblance of Heart Rate Reactions to Laboratory Stress

One of the best ways to examine family resemblance is by studying twins. This allows the researcher not only to examine how similar family members are for a given characteristic, but also to explore the origins of their similarity, whether it arises from shared environmental experience or as a result of similar genetic make-up. If identical, or monozygotic (MZ) twins are more similar with regard to a given characteristic than non-identical or dizygotic (DZ) twins then we have good grounds for suspecting that genetic factors make a strong contribution to the characteristic. We infer this from the knowledge that MZ twins are genetically identical, whereas DZ twins on average share only half their genes in common.

Early twin studies of cardiac activity during psychological stress (Shapiro *et al.*, 1968; Theorell *et al.*, 1979), although reporting data broadly suggestive of genetic involvement, employed either too few subjects or insufficiently sophisticated analytical techniques to afford clear conclusions. More recently, Carroll *et al.* (1985) recorded the heart rate reactions of forty MZ and forty DZ pairs of young male twins to the video game stress. Analysis of the level of resemblance of heart rate reactions between the two sorts of twins revealed substantial resemblance between MZ twin pair members, but little or no correspondence between DZ twin pair members. More sophisticated analysis revealed that individual variation in heart rate reactions, as would be expected from the above, had a sizeable genetic component. Approximately half of the variation among people in heart rate reactions to stress, analysis of the data from this study implied, was attributable to their genetic make-up. Subsequent research largely bears out this conclusion. It would appear, then, that how the heart reacts to psychological stress depends very much on our biological make-up; some individuals appear primed biologically to respond with large-magnitude, metabolically exaggerated cardiac reactions.

Cardiac Reactions to Stress in High Risk Individuals

A number of studies have now compared the cardiac reactions of individuals at risk for hypertension, as a result of having parents with high blood pressure, with those of individuals without such risk. These have been reviewed recently by Fredrikson and Matthews (1990). Although exceptions exist, there is broad agreement that the offspring of parents with high blood pressure show larger magnitude heart rate reactions than the offspring of normotensive parents, but only to 'active coping' stressors. One study might usefully serve as an illustration. Carroll *et al.* (1985) managed to contact the parents of the young twins whose cardiac reactions they had monitored in the laboratory in fifty-nine out of the eighty cases. The parents were interviewed in their homes about their health, medication, etc., and their blood pressures were measured. Two readings were taken, one at the beginning and one at the end of the visit. Parental blood pressure and general health assessment indicated that in eleven families both parents presented at least marginally high blood pressures across the two readings (had systolic blood pressure greater than or equal to 140 mm/Hg and/or diastolic blood pressure greater than or equal to 90 mm/Hg), or were currently receiving anti-hypertensive medication. The average heart rate reaction of their offspring (11.6 beats per minute) was significantly higher than that recorded for the rest of the sample (6.2 beats per minute).

Frederikson and Matthews (1990) have also reviewed a number of studies where risk has been defined by the blood pressure status of the subject rather than that of parents. Essentially, young subjects with high, but sub-hypertensive, blood pressure have been compared with subjects who are unambiguously normotensive. For heart rate reactions to active stressors, the results are unequivocal; at-risk subjects show consistently larger magnitude reactions. Not only that, but recent evidence indicates that these larger-magnitude heart rate reactions occur in the absence of any commensurate relative rise in energy expenditure. In a study reported by Sims and Carroll (1990), heart rate and oxygen consumption were monitored during mental arithmetic stress, and also during graded physical exercise, in a group of young men with mildly elevated but sub-hypertensive blood pressure levels, and also in unambiguously normotensive subjects. Greater heart rate increases to the stress were observed in the former group, and the group difference in heart rate could not be explained by variation in energy expenditure. When the exercise data were used to enable the heart rate reactions to mental stress to be expressed in terms of heart rate 'additional' to energy expenditure, the group difference persisted. The mildly high blood pressure subjects showed greater 'additional' heart rate reactions than the normotensives. In a subsequent study, Carroll, Harris and Cross (1991) monitored cardiac output in analogous groups of subjects at rest and while they engaged in mental arithmetic stress and graded bicycle exercise. Applying the same methodology as above to yield measures of 'additional' cardiac output, substantially greater 'additional' cardiac output reactions were observed in the subjects with mildly elevated blood pressures than in their normotensive counterparts.

While these high risk studies yield data that would seem to implicate metabolically exaggerated cardiac reactions in the development of essential hypertension, caution is warranted. Definitive evidence awaits the outcome of longitudinal studies where the blood pressures of normotensive young people, whose cardiovascular reactions to stress have been monitored at the outset of the study, are tracked over years, if not decades. No such longitudinal data are as yet available. The study which most closely conforms to this design is one conducted by Falkner and her associates (Falkner *et al.*, 1984). Using a mental arithmetic stressor, the cardiovascular reactions of fifty adolescents with elevated blood pressure were monitored at the outset of the study. The reactions of a normotensive control group were also monitored. Subjects were then followed up for a period of up to forty-one months, during which time twenty-eight of the fifty adolescents had developed essential hypertension proper. It was found that these subjects were more likely to have a positive family history of hypertension. In addition, they were also the subjects who displayed the most marked heart rate and blood pressure reaction to the initial mental arithmetic stress test, a result certainly in line with the proposition that excessive cardiovascular reactivity in the face of psychological stress is pathogenic.

While the foregoing account has focused on the role of cardiovascular, and in particular cardiac, reactions to stress in the development of hypertension, it would be wrong to leave the reader with the impression that this is the only important contributing mechanism.

Blood Pressure and the Renal Excretion of Salt and Water

Several authorities have also implicated the kidneys in the development of high blood pressure. Given their role as principal agents in controlling the body's fluid balance and the relationship between volume and pressure this is hardly surprising. A key mechanism here is that of pressure diuresis. Put simply, when blood pressure increases, the kidneys normally respond by increasing the excretion of salt and water which results in a lowering of blood pressure. Recent evidence suggests that stress may compromise the functioning of this renal pressure diuresis process.

Studies conducted at the University of North Carolina by Light and her colleagues (e.g., Light *et al.*, 1983), first in dogs and later in humans, indicated that psychological stress can provoke salt and fluid retention rather than excretion, and thus the usual blood pressure corrective process fails to operate in such circumstances. In the first of this series of studies, six dogs were exposed to treadmill exercise and then to the psychological stress of an electric shock avoidance task. While exercise led to the predicted increase in salt and water excretion, the behavioural stress task led to decreased excretion. These changes in opposite directions occurred even though blood pressure and heart rate rose by similar amounts in the two tasks. Further marked individual variation was noted among these dogs in terms of their renal reaction to the stress of attempting to avoid an impending electric shock; only three of the dogs showed substantial retention of salt and fluid. Interestingly, it was these three dogs which also showed the greatest heart rate reactions to the behavioural stress.

In a subsequent study, thirteen young men at risk for hypertension, either as a result of family history or because of already elevated systolic blood pressure levels, had their salt and water excretion levels measured at rest and during the stress of a competitive reaction time task, where reactions faster than criterion carried monetary rewards. Eleven not-at-risk subjects were tested under the same conditions. Heart rate was also recorded and subjects were designated as high and low heart rate reactors on the basis of their reactions to the competition stress. Both heart rate reactivity and risk of hypertension interacted to affect the excretory reactions of these young people. Briefly, high risk subjects who were high heart rate reactors showed salt and water retention in the face of the psychological stress; all other subjects displayed the conventional diuretic response. This subgroup also tended to show the most prolonged blood pressure elevations during the study. Thus perhaps, abnormal cardiac and renal reactions to stress might be the products of a common mechanism in some dogs and humans, which confers on them a particular risk for hypertension. While one should be careful not to claim too much on the basis of what is after all rather small-scale research using a time-consuming and difficult methodology, the interaction of cardiac and renal reactions to stress is certainly an area worth further study.

Concluding Remarks

There is now evidence to indicate that some people, faced with psychological stresses and challenges, respond with cardiac reactions that are excessive in terms of their concurrent levels of energy expenditure. Such 'additional' reactions have been demonstrated with regard to both heart rate and, more recently, cardiac output. There is also evidence that excessive cardiac reactivity may be a stable feature of some individuals, with a sizeable genetic component. Most importantly, 'additional' cardiac reactions to stress seem to be a particular feature of young individuals who as a result of their family history or current blood pressure status are particularly at risk for developing hypertension. Thus, there are reasons for implicating large-magnitude, excessive cardiac reactions to stress in the development of hypertension. However, this is unlikely to be the whole story, and there is emerging evidence that the kidneys are susceptible to stress in a manner which suggests that they too might be part of the process through which stress exerts an influence.

As with CHD, hypertension is a multi-faceted disorder with a complex aetiology. In addition to reactivity to stress, features such as diet and, in particular, the excessive consumption of salt in individuals with a particular sensitivity, and behavioural styles, especially those involving the suppression of anger, also seem to be involved. The current chapter has dealt only with parts of the story; a complete account will undoubtedly have to integrate a whole host of factors and processes, both psychological and biological.

Chapter 4

Cancer and the Immune System

In the preceding chapters consideration was given to the effects of stress on the cardiovascular system and their implications for cardiovascular pathology. Evidence was presented that excessive cardiovascular reactions to psychological stress may be implicated, along with perhaps renal responses to stress, in the development of essential hypertension. Hypertension, as indicated, is a known risk factor for potentially lethal cardiovascular disorders, including CHD. We also noted that a major behavioural contributor to CHD, the type A behaviour pattern may exert its influence by increasing the frequency of a person's encounters with stress. Accordingly, stress and cardiovascular pathology would appear to be inextricably linked through the impact that stress has on the cardiovascular system.

That stress affects cardiovascular functioning is, however, hardly a contemporary relevation; acknowledgment of such effects can be traced to the writings of the great physicians of antiquity, such as Galen in the first century AD. In contrast, it is only in very recent times that we have come to realize that stress influences another area of the bodily functioning: the immune system. The potential implications of this influence for disease is only just starting to be appreciated.

In this chapter I shall describe some of the evidence that links stress to the responsiveness of the immune system and then turn to the possible implications that stress, as a result, might hold for cancer.

The Immune System

First of all, though, let us consider the purpose of the immune system and how, in general terms, it functions. The immune system affords us protection against noxious agents, from viruses, bacteria, mutated and abnormal cells, and allergens. It comes into play when our external defences (the skin and the mucociliary systems in the nose and lungs) have been breached. It is a tall order, for although most people are born with some natural immunities, the vast bulk of our immunities are acquired. Thus the immune system has to learn to discriminate that which properly belongs to the body, is part of 'self', from what is an intrusion. Such 'non-self' agents are generally referred to as antigens. So abnormal cancer cells, bacteria, viruses, and even pollen are all examples of antigens and all trigger the immune system into reaction. The major players in this immune reaction are the lymphocytes, or white blood cells, which are produced by the bone marrow. There are two types of lymphocyte, the B-cells and T-cells. When an antigen invades the body the B-cells, upon making contact with it, produce proteins called antibodies to combat the intruder. These antibodies are made up of five types of immuno-globulin (Ig), each with its own particular mode of action; for example, whereas IgG functions to cover antigens with a substance that permits their destruction by other immune cells, IgM is mainly effective against bacteria. The ability of the B-cells to produce antibodies in the face of a particular anti-gen depends on their previous acquaintance with the antigen. It is on the basis of recognition that the B-cells can produce the required antibodies and an acquired immune reaction can take place to neutralize the intrusion.

The T-cells assist either through coordinating the B-cell response or by attacking and destroying antigens directly. Because this latter function is part of a natural and largely non-specific reaction, not the result of an acquired response stemming from prior acquaintance, some T-cells are referred to as natural killer cells. The coordinating T-cells are of two kinds: helper cells which activate the B-cells and suppressor cells which inhibit B-cell activity. These are the bare bones of what is not only a complex system, but one that is essential to the body's integrity.

Stress and Immune Function

There is now substantial evidence that a variety of stresses (high intensity noise, physical restraint, inescapable electric shock) reduce the competency of the immune system in mice. However, for the present let us focus on humans. Here, too, evidence is accumulating that stress can impair immune functioning. A number of studies can be cited in support. Some of the most impressive have been conducted by Janice Kiecolt-Glaser and her colleagues. For example, Kiecolt-Glaser *et al.* (1986) obtained blood samples from medical student volunteers one month before their examinations, and again on the second day of the examinations. Analysis of these samples revealed a significant decline in the working efficiency of several components of the immune system with examination stress. For example, there were reliable reductions in the percentage of T-helper lymphocytes and in natural killer cell activity during the examination relative to the earlier baseline assessment. In a subsequent study Kiecolt-Glaser *et al.* (1987) investigated the effect of marital disruption on immunological function. It has long been argued that marriage and the quality of marriage are important factors in psychological and physical well-being. Divorced and separated individuals have been observed to have poorer mental and physical health than comparable married, widowed or single indivi-duals. For example, divorced and separated individuals are disproportionately represented in both inpatient and outpatient psychiatric populations. Further, marital disruption is a powerful predictor of physical illness, with separated individuals suffering from more acute illnesses and visiting their doctors far more often than married people. In this study, blood samples were obtained from thirty-eight married women and from thirty-eight comparable separated or divorced women. All of this latter group had been separated within the previous six years, and sixteen of them had been separated within the last year. In addition, the married group were administered a questionnaire to assess the quality of their marriage. While there was no overall difference between the two groups in immune functioning, analysis of the sixteen recently separated women did reveal striking differences. For example the recently separated women had reliably lower percentages of natural killer cells and T-helper lymphocytes than their married counterparts. With regard to the issue of marital quality among the married women, the researchers found that the poorer the self-reported quality of the marriage, the less the immune reaction to an introduced antigen.

A contemporary Swedish study provides independent support. Arnetz *et al.* (1987) investigated the impact of unemployment on immune function. Several areas of evidence implicate unemployment in poor physical and psychological well-being. This is perhaps hardly surprising when one considers the complex social functions that employment fulfils in our society, aside from the financial benefit that accrues. For example, Jahoda and Rush (1980) listed five such functions, which they argued are only properly satisfied by paid employment, i.e., charitable work or leisure activities might fulfil some of these functions but cannot satisfy all of them. First of all, work imposes a definitive time structure on the day. Second, work demands social contact, and third, it requires that the individual cooperates with these contacts in order to achieve collective goals. Fourth, work confers an identity and social status on an individual. Finally, work requires people to be active. With job loss, these important social advantages are also lost. The focus of the study by Arnetz *et al.* was a sample of recently unemployed women. They were divided into two groups. Members of both groups were in receipt of full benefit, i.e., 90 per cent of their previous income, under the Swedish welfare system; thus material deprivation, which in so many countries is the condition of the unemployed, was not an issue in this study. In addition, one of the two groups of subjects was given the opportunity to participate in a political and social self-help programme, in order to try to counter the stigma and inactivity that so often appear to be the lot of the unemployed. A final group, comprising women in stable employment, served as a control. Blood samples were taken at various intervals during the first twelve months of unemployment in the former two groups, and at comparable intervals in the control groups. While the groups did not vary in terms of B and T cells throughout the period of observation, there were differences in immune reaction to an antigen. After nine months of unemployment there was a decrease in reactivity, whereas the employed control group of women showed no change over time. This effect was somewhat more marked for the unemployment group not given access to the psychosocial programme, but was still, to an extent, evident in the intervention group. In sum, the results of this study suggest that unemployment, even in the absence of financial penalty, still has implications for the efficient working of the immune system, and that this effect is only very modestly affected by a psychosocial intervention programme. Thus we can add unemployment to the growing catalogue of stressors with implications for immune function. It is worth the reader noting, though, that not all of these stressors affect the immune system in the same fashion. As a consequence, it is possible that different stressors may have varying pathological implications. It is also possibly worth recording that the consumption of alcohol ad caffeine tends to rise during periods of stress, and excessive consumption of both substances appears to have detrimental effects on several aspects of immune functioning. However, the stress effects described above are difficult, if not impossible, to explain solely by reference to alcohol and caffeine abuse.

Although the evidence from research on mice points to a fair degree of adaptation with persistent stress exposure, and consequent recovery of immune system efficiency, evidence from the study of humans exposed to more chronic stress paints a somewhat bleaker picture. For more than a decade now, Andrew Baum and his associates have been investigating the human consequences of the accident at the Three Mile Island nuclear installation. Among these various studies is one that explored immune functioning. A small sample of people living near the installation still exhibiting symptoms of stress some six years after the incident were compared with a group of control subjects. Among other things, the Three Mile Island sample were characterized by a reduced number of B-cells and natural killer cells (see Gatchel *et al.*, 1989).

Cancer and Stress

Let us now turn to the possible implications of these effects for pathology and in particular for cancer. While reductions in immune system efficiency are likely to influence the susceptibility to a range of disorders from infectious disease to allergies, it is beyond the scope of this text to address all of these possible sequelae. Since it is, by far, the most researched condition, attention will focus on cancer. In addition, arguments of a link between cancer and psychological disposition have a substantial historical pedigree. Again, Galen in the first century AD was perhaps the earliest proponent of a link. It seems that so much in Galen's early writings, at least in terms of general advocacy, if not in terms of particular processes, resonates with contemporary health psychology.

Since there are more than a hundred different forms of cancer, it is highly unlikely that one particular set of processes will prove responsible for all. Nevertheless, general theories of cancer development, that purport to account for many cancerous growths, have been put forward. Most relevant to the current tack is the idea that the starting point for cancer is genetic defects within cells which prompt mutations in cell development. It remains possible that psychological stress plays a triggering role in this process. More probably, though, stress has its impact on subsequent mutagenic development. As indicated, the key role of the immune system is to recognize and combat 'non-self' matter. These surveillance and defence functions undoubtedly extend to mutagenic cells, which will be regarded by the system as alien and 'non-self'. Under normal conditions cell mutations will be recognized and dealt with. However, if the immune system is operating at less than optimal efficiency, as a result, as we have seen, of psychological stress, it may fail to detect malignant cells and thus their proliferation and the development of a tumour will go unchecked. Of the various components of the immune system, it has been argued recently (Greer and Brady, 1988), natural killer cells may play a key part, because they require no previous exposure to their target, and are capable of reacting rapidly to a wide range of malignancies. There is certainly evidence in line with this. For example, individuals at risk of cancer, as a result of high family incidence of cancer, have lower natural killer cell activity than low risk control subjects. Two sorts of evidence on the relationship between stress and cancer need to be considered: animal studies and research with humans.

Cancer and Stress in Animals

Again mice have proved a popular species for study, and the evidence certainly suggests that environmental stress influences the progress of tumour growth. However, it cannot be considered as establishing that stress is a cancer trigger. Nevertheless, it is broadly consistent with the theory outlined above.

Let me briefly illustrate. In an early study, Sakakibara (1966) exposed mice to a variety of different lighting conditions, either a normal dark/light cycle, continuous light, continuous dark, or a bright, flashing light for eight hours a day. This latter condition was undoubtedly the most stressful. The mice received a carcinogenic chemical and the progress of tumour growth was measured over a period of twenty weeks. Tumours developed most rapidly in the mice exposed to flashing lights and almost 80 per cent of that group actually developed tumours. Continuous light, probably the next most stressful condition, was associated with tumour development in 60 per cent of mice, while the analogous figure for continuous darkness was 36 per cent. Only 24 per cent of mice kept in normal lighting conditions developed tumours. Other stressful environmental conditions appear to have similar pathogenic effects. For example, Henry *et al.* (1975) reported that the stress of social isolation produced relatively rapid tumour development in mice. Finally, Riley *et al.* (1981) observed that mice that had been exposed to a variety of stressors died at a much greater rate following implantation of a tumour than mice previously kept in low stress conditions. Twenty-five days after implantation more than 80 per cent of the previously stressed mice had died compared to only 40 per cent of their low stress counterparts.

Cancer and Stress in Humans

While the search for psychological factors in human cancer can be regarded as a search for gold, so often the product has been much baser metal. Some of the reasons for this we shall consider at the end of this chapter. Nevertheless, a few persistent themes seem to emerge from research in this field.

First of all, of the various stressful life events that have been examined as potential precursors of cancer, absence or loss of a close relationship emerges most consistently. For example, Scherg and Blohmke (1988) reported a study comparing the life events of two groups of women who had undergone gynaecological examination: a group of over 500 women who were revealed by the examination to be suffering from a variety of cancers and a group of 1,500 women who were revealed at examination to be cancer-free. Of the life events examined, three, in descending order of importance, were most predictive of cancer. These were: death of mother in childhood; divorced, widowed or separated at any time; at least one traumatic World War Two experience. This fits well with the frequently attested clinical observation that the absence or loss of a close relationship is frequently a characteristic of cancer patients. It is worth mentioning here that bereavement has been found to be associated with reduced immune system efficiency. Schleifer *et al.* (1980) assessed the immune functioning of a small group of men whose wives were dying. Assessments were made before the spouse's death and after. Immune reactions to antigens were significantly poorer after the spouse's death than before. Irwin (1988) reports a couple of more recent studies that add to the picture. Immune system functioning was compared for three groups of women: those whose husbands were dying of lung cancer; women whose husbands had recently died; those whose husbands were in good health. Psychological adjustment was measured by a rating scale and women who were anticipating the death of their spouse or had already experienced it had poorer ratings than those with healthy husbands. Further, those with poorer adjustment were found to have reduced natural killer cell activity. In addition, symptoms of depression were also greater in these subjects. In a second longitudinal study, focusing on bereaved women and assessing immune function and depression before and after bereavement, reduction in natural killer cell activity was strongly related to an increase in depressive symptoms. It would appear that the loss of an important plank in an individual's social support system has implications for the efficiency with which the immune system reacts to challenge, and, as a consequence, possibly for cancer too. In an early prospective study, Thomas and Duszynski (1974) explored the role of such social support in affording protection against a range of conditions, including cancer. Almost a thousand medical students were interviewed at the outset and then followed up for between ten and fifteen years. Those who had developed cancer by follow-up reported the absence of close family ties.

Cancer and Depression

It could be argued that a common thread in all of this is depression, i.e., that the particular life events and circumstances that appear to be implicated in cancer, the loss or absence of a close relationship, are likely to promote depression, and it is the psychological state of depression which predisposes the individual to cancer. Again, it is important to record that there is evidence that depression is associated with reduced immune system responsiveness (see, e.g., Dantzer and Kelley, 1989), as well as a substantial amount of clinical case reports of an association between cancer and depressed mood. There is also some, more systematic, evidence of a link. Jansen and Muenz (1984) in a retrospective study compared women with breast cancer, healthy women and women with non-malignant disease. A number of questionnaires were administered. The women with breast cancer were characterized by substantially more feelings of depression than women in the other two groups, as well as being substantially less demonstrative.

More impressive, through, are the results from a prospective study conducted among male employees at the Western Electric Company near Chicago. Those employed for at least two years in 1957–8 formed the focus of the study. Shekelle *et al.* (1981) reported on 2,020 of these men seventeen years later. Various aspects of psychological disposition had been measured at the outset. What emerged after seventeen years was a significant association between questionnaire depression scores and death from cancer; those with high depression scores were twice as likely to have died from cancer over the seventeen-year period. The most recent report on this study (Persky *et al.*, 1987) details the findings twenty years on from initial assessment. By this time a total of 212 of these men had cancer. Again a relationship was found between cancer and depression, both for incidence of cancer and mortality. The association persisted even when age, cigarette smoking, alcohol consumption, occupational status within the company, and family history of cancer were taken into account.

While this result is compelling, it has to be conceded that several other studies have failed to find a relationship between cancer and depression. This is particularly the case in studies which have focused on clinically depressed patients. For example, Watson and Schuld (1977) compared the psychiatric diagnoses and questionnaire depression scores of psychiatric patients who later developed cancers with those who developed either no disease or benign growths. At least two years had to have elapsed between psychiatric assessment and disease diagnosis. Watson and Schuld found no difference among the groups either in terms of diagnosis (i.e., there were no greater numbers of depressives in the cancer group) or in terms of questionnaire depression scores. While findings such as these might be considered a problem for a cancer-depression link, it is possible that they serve mainly to refine just what that link is, rather than argue against any sort of link at all. Thus, instead of a major contribution to cancer by stress or by severe depression, it is perhaps the interaction between life events and coping style that is important. In this context, it may be the reaction to significant loss in one's life, be it a depressive reaction or a reaction of hopelessness that is particularly implicated.

Cancer and Behavioural Style

What may be significant, then, is the way we behave in the face of particular life events, such as bereavement. Depression is one such reaction. However, might it not represent a particular instance of what may be a more pervasive pathogenic orientation towards stressful events, i.e., might there be a general cancer-prone behavioural style, analogous to coronary-prone type A behaviour?

A number of threads of evidence seem to suggest, at least to some researchers in the field, that many cancer patients are characterized by just such a behavioural pattern. The earliest suggestive studies were conducted by Kissen. For example, Kissen (1963) investigated 161 men with lung cancer and a comparably sized control group of men with other pulmonary diseases. Questionnaire responses revealed that the cancer patients suffered from diminished emotional expression both in childhood and in their present adult lives. In a more recent study, Dattore *et al.* (1980) compared male hospital patients with cancer and matched non-cancer control patients. Those with cancer showed greater repression of feelings. Perhaps the most impressive evidence of an association between emotional suppression and cancer stems from the research of Steven Greer and his associates in London. Their focus has been breast cancer and the suppression of one particular affective state, anger. In their earliest study (Greer and Morris, 1975), women subsequently found to have breast cancer at biopsy were compared with women subsequently revealed to have benign breast disease. Comparison of the two groups' pre-biopsy behavioural propensities revealed that the former group reported an abnormal pattern of emotional behaviour; specifically, they showed extreme suppression of anger. This was most noticeably the case in younger patients, i.e., those under the age of 50. In a more recent attempt to replicate this result, Morris *et al.* (1981) again interviewed and administered questionnaires to women prior to biopsy. Those with breast cancer were compared to those without, as before. Again, the former group reported experiencing and displaying anger to a far less extent, and again this effect was more noticeable in the younger group. In addition, these young cancer patients were more likely to use denial in the face of stress. Jansen and Muenz (1984) in the study cited earlier also found evidence of anger suppression.

Thus what seems to characterize the pre-morbid personal styles of cancer patients is a broad suppression of active emotional display, which represents itself in several studies as the stifling of anger expression. In the face of personal loss, though, it is plausible that such suppression is manifest as hopelessness and depression, two of the most non-demonstrative affective dispositions. Finally there is some, albeit preliminary, evidence of a link between emotional suppression and immunological functioning. Pettingale *et al.* (1977) report on association between the tendency to suppress anger and serum immunoglobulin levels.

Denial and Prognosis

As we shall see, one of the major difficulties facing research in this area is deciphering cause from effect. Are these psychological characteristics contributing factors in the development of cancer or are they a reaction to its development, or are both products of some superordinate cause, e.g., genetic disposition? We shall return to this in a minute, as well as listing some of the other nagging problems.

First of all, though, it is important to appreciate that psychological factors may not only play a part in the aetiology of cancer, but also in the patient's subsequent fate, for there is growing evidence that the coping strategy that patients adopt in dealing with the disease has implications for prognosis. Two examples might usefully serve to illustrate. Pettingale *et al.* (1985) characterized four broad styles of coping strategies from women's responses in interviews conducted four months after mastectomy. These were 'stoic acceptance', 'denial', 'fighting spirit', and 'helplessness, hopelessness'. Examination five years after the operation indicated that coping strategy was related to recurrence-free survival. Patients who adopted either the 'denial' or 'fighting spirit' approaches fared much better. In addition, Pettingale *et al.* (1981) found that immunoglobulin levels were higher in patients coping with an attitude of denial than in those adopting other strategies. Since this finding has undoubted implications for counselling and therapy, it is worthy of replication. However, only one study to date has attempted to confirm these results. Dean and Surtees (1989) again interviewed women with breast cancer three months after mastectomy, and allocated them, on the basis of their interview responses, to one of the four previously mentioned coping strategies. Outcome at between six and eight years following the operation was then examined in terms of the strategy the patient indicated she had adopted. Only denial emerged from the analysis as offering an advantage in terms of disease recurrence or mortality. Fighting spirit could not be distinguished from the two other relatively unsuccessful strategies, stoic acceptance and helplessness/hopelessness. Dean and Surtees urge caution, though, since they experienced some difficulty in measuring coping strategy and found evidence of variation in strategy over time. Certainly, there is evidence that cancer patients' emotional reactions to their situation vary markedly with time (B.L. Anderson *et al.*, 1989).

Increasingly, programmes of psychological support are being advocated for cancer patients. That is undoubtedly no bad thing. As B.L. Anderson (1989) points out, such programmes can directly improve the psychological adjustment of cancer patients and perhaps even have some positive effect on disease outcome. However, what the common finding from these two studies, that denial may be beneficial, suggests is that such programmes should take care not to undermine the patient's defence system where it is likely to be of benefit. What is perhaps required, as Cull (1990) suggests, is a selective service, targeted at patients with marked psychological problems.

This chapter has concentrated for the most part on possible psychological antecedents of cancer. However, it is probable that the most important role for health psychology will be in devising and researching ways of dealing with the psychological consequences of cancer, ways of fostering generally better prognoses, and of improving the quality of life of cancer patients.

Concluding Remarks

As indicated previously, the search for psychological factors implicated in cancer is fraught with difficulties. There is the issue of cause and effect. Are implicated psychological factors truly antecedent or are they consequences of a diagnosis of cancer? With research that is retrospective, i.e., compares already diagnosed patients with other non-cancer patients or healthy controls, it is impossible to resolve this issue. Even in some prospective research such as that by Greer and his associates where psychological assessment was conducted prior to definitive diagnostic examination, i.e., biopsy, and women subsequently revealed to have malignancies were compared to those revealed to have benign disease, problems remain. It is still possible that it is the malignant tumour development, whether diagnosed or not, that affects psychological disposition. If this is the case, then it is important to establish just when the malignant growth started. However, it is extremely difficult to establish precisely when the cancer started to grow; it is certainly unreliable to make presumptions of disease onset from the date of diagnosis. Finally, even in properly prospective studies like that undertaken at the Western Electric Company, where subjects undertook psychological assessment in the 1950s and had their health tracked for the next twenty years, another difficulty exists: it is not at all certain that subjects' psychological disposition and behavioural style will remain static over twenty years of follow-up.

In addition, it is important to recognize that cancer is not a unitary disease. While psychological factors may be important in some, they may be largely irrelevant to others. For example, in concluding his review of the earlier research on psychological factors in cancer, Fox (1978) makes the following distinction. Cancers in children and young adults, he argued, are probably genetic in origin, whereas cancers in the elderly probably reflect increased exposure over time to physical carcinogenic agents and/or a lowered threshold for susceptibility. The latter is seen as stemming from an impaired immune reaction, which may simply reflect the aging process or possibly arise from the cumulative impact of psychological stress. However, it is cancers in middle age, i.e., between 35 and 55 years, Fox suggests, that are most likely to be a function, at least in part, of psychological factors.

At this stage then, we must be careful not to overstate the role of psychological factors in either the onset or the course of cancer, nor to place too high a faith in possible amelioration of the disease through psychological means. While the current data suggest that psychological factors are involved in some cancers, and that coping style affects prognosis, there is still a long way to go. The precise nature and extent of any such influence remains to be determined, as does any resultant implications for therapy and disease management. I have tried to abstract the most consistent themes from the available research, but readily acknowledge that substantial confirmation is required before it can be asserted with proper confidence that psychological forces play a major role.

Chapter 5

The Challenge of AIDS

In the space of little more than a decade, Acquired Immune Deficiency Syndrome (AIDS) has emerged as probably the most challenging medical and social issue of our time. As Phillips and White (1991) have pointed out, it is now barely credible that as recently as 1980, AIDS was essentially unknown. Its subsequent trajectory, though, has meant that it is now at the top of the global health agenda.

As with cancer, AIDS involves the immune system, although in a different manner. It is the consequence of infection by the human immunodeficiency virus (HIV) which attacks the immune system itself. Thus, HIV actually targets that very system within the body which is concerned with guarding against viral infection. It is this which renders HIV so toxic. A number of immunological effects have been attributed to HIV, among which are reductions in T-lymphocytes, including the T-helper cells and some immunoglobulins, and reduced responsiveness of cells to antigens. With immune competency seriously compromised, the body is vulnerable to opportunistic attack by other infections and cancers.

However, it is important to stress that HIV infection and AIDS are not the same thing. In the vast majority of cases HIV infection is symptomless. In some people, though, infection brings with it a variety of symptoms which can include swollen glands, weight loss, fever or diarrhoea. These are referred to as the AIDS-related complex or ARC. It is often viewed as an intermediate stage between HIV infection and full-blown AIDS. Reductions in immunological competence can be detected with ARC, but diagnosis of AIDS requires the additional identification of an opportunistic infection or a cancer not usually associated with individuals who have intact immune systems. Among these are a form of pneumonia (Pneumocystis Carinii) and a rare variety of skin cancer (Kaposi's sarcoma). It is these, along with tumours of the lymphatic system, that cause most of the fatalities among AIDS sufferers.

HIV displays varying and occasionally protracted periods of dormancy. Infected individuals can remain symptomless for several years. The current best estimates of progression times from HIV infection to AIDS indicate an average incubation period of around ten years (Chin, 1990). Twenty per cent of infected individuals develop AIDS within five years, and 50 per cent within ten years. While no data are currently available beyond ten years, the World Health Organization (WHO) calculates that 75 per cent of HIV-infected individuals will progress to AIDS within fifteen years, and by twenty years 95 per cent of all those infected will have developed AIDS. While progression rates do not seem to vary much from country to country or with mode of transmission of HIV, some differences have been recorded. Preliminary evidence suggests that children born with the HIV virus develop AIDS at a much quicker rate. Chin (1990) assesses that 25 per cent develop AIDS within the first year of life and that by the end of the fourth year of life, some 80 per cent of those who have been infected prenatally will have developed AIDS. Further, Mulleady (1987) indicates that intravenous (IV) drug users with AIDS appear to show a higher incidence of pneumonia compared with homosexual men, while the latter show a higher incidence of Kaposi's sarcoma. Since the average survival with pneumonia is ten months compared with fifteen to eighteen months for Kaposi's sarcoma, this suggests that survival time after diagnosis for IV drug users will be slightly less than that for homosexual men.

Incidence of AIDS and HIV Infection

The trajectory for HIV infection and AIDS is so steep that estimated incidences are no sooner published than they are overtaken. For example, Gatchel *et al.* (1989) reported one early study of homosexual men in San Francisco where the incidence of HIV infection in 1978 was less than 10 per cent but by 1985 was more than 75 per cent. Current estimates in the USA indicate that around 150,000 have been diagnosed as having AIDS, of whom around 90,000 have already died of the disease. Blacks and Hispanics are disproportionately represented in these figures; they are currently twice as likely as the general American population to contract AIDS. It is estimated that over 1,500,000 Americans are infected with HIV. In the UK there have now been over 3,000 cases of AIDS, over half of which have already died, and at least 10,000 people are estimated to be HIV-positive, although the actual figure could be much higher. In both countries, AIDS has been far more common among men than women, but the incidence of the disease in women is starting to rise sharply, as are estimates of their numbers infected with HIV.

The WHO estimates that globally more than half a million people have contracted AIDS, although only around half that number of cases are officially confirmed. It is clear that there is substantial under-reporting. Over 150 countries have reported cases of AIDS. Moreover, the WHO estimates that some ten million people world-wide are infected with HIV, and have recently revised their estimates of the cumulative disease incidence by the end of the decade from three million to four million. By far the region of greatest prevalence in the world is the countries of sub-Saharan Africa. In addition, since the mode of transmission there has been almost exclusively that of heterosexual sexual intercourse, as many, if not more, women are affected as men. Chin (1990) estimates that some two and a half million women in sub-Sarahan Africa had been infected by HIV by the end of the 1980s, and some 225,000 had already developed AIDS. The projections for 1992 indicate the rate of spread. Some four million women were predicted to have been infected by the virus by then, and the cumulative AIDS total was predicted to be 600,000. Since the bulk of such women were and are of child-bearing age this clearly has massive implications for infection and AIDS in children. While in the West we are only beginning to be confronted with the problem of children being infected with HIV prenatally from infected mothers, Chin reckoned that by the end of the 1980s HIV infection was the lot of some half a million children, and the figure was estimated to rise to one million by 1992. The corresponding figures for AIDS were 290,000 and 600,000 respectively. During the late 1980s in many central African cities, 5 to 10 per cent of all infants were HIV-positive. These figures give some idea of the pandemic character of the disease. As one might expect, AIDS is by far the single largest cause of premature death in most sub-Saharan African countries. The same is true of New York City, where AIDS is the leading cause of death among 20-to-40-year-olds.

Transmission of HIV

Despite the now epidemic proportions of AIDS, HIV is a relatively poorly transmitted virus. While HIV has been detected in a range of body fluids, it is through the exchange of sexual fluids or of blood or blood products (by IV drug users sharing needles, through contaminated blood transfusion, or prenatal exchange from mother to child) that HIV passes from an infected to a non-infected individual. There are no cases where the virus has been spread through other bodily fluids such as saliva or tears. Nor is there any instance of HIV being transmitted by casual contacts such as kissing or touching, nor through the sharing of drinking and eating utensils. Finally, studies of infected haemophiliacs and their partners indicate that sexual intercourse with an infected person does not inevitably result in the transmission of infection. It increasingly appears to be the case that ease of transmission in such circumstances is dependent on the activity status of the virus.

In the West, AIDS was originally identified in homosexual and bisexual men and located in epicentres such as San Francisco and New York. It was subsequently detected in haemophiliacs and others who had received contaminated blood transfusions, and in IV drug users as a result of needle sharing. These initial manifestations led to a number of misconceptions and inappropriate and damaging moral posturings. First, these early victims of the disease in the West were frequently characterized as innocent and unfortunate (e.g., haemophiliacs) and, by implication, culpable and deserving of the disease (homosexual men, IV drug users). It is likely that in some areas, such attributions prevented the early mobilization of appropriate health care, educational and research provision. Second, in groups already subject to prejudice and discrimination (e.g., homosexual men), high initial AIDS prevalence served to compound social injustice and victimization. Third, while AIDS was focused in particular on risk groups, mistaken beliefs about the invulnerability of others, particularly heterosexuals who did not inject drugs, could gain currency. Examination of the situation in central Africa would have quickly dispelled such illusions. There heterosexual sexual transmission is the main route of transmission, and heterosexuals the main victims of the disease. Although, in the West, homosexual and bisexual men still predominate in the AIDS statistics, they are rapidly being caught up by IV drug users and, in some areas, the latter constitute the major group of sufferers. In addition, particularly in the USA, where the disease has had longer to develop than in other western countries, there are increasing numbers of heterosexual men and women contracting AIDS. Thus, heterosexual transmission of HIV is rapidly increasing in the West, as is the prenatal transmission from mother to child. Phillips and White (1991) have argued that these early mythologies about AIDS and its identification with particular 'deviant' or marginal groups very much acted as an obstacle to the adoption of behaviours in the population as a whole which would limit the further spread of HIV.

Responses to AIDS

There is, as yet, no medical cure for AIDS, nor has a vaccine to combat HIV infection been developed. At the time of writing, neither appear to be likely in the immediate future. One particular drug, AZT, has been used widely with AIDS sufferers and research does seem to indicate that it retards the progress of AIDS and increases life expectancy. Nevertheless, AZT is not a cure, and once an individual develops AIDS the prognosis is poor, with or without AZT.

Currently, then, the only available strategy against AIDS is to limit the spread of HIV within the population, which can only be achieved by persuading individuals to adopt behaviours that are likely to minimize the possibilities of virus transmission. Two behaviours which render individuals particularly at risk are the sharing of needles among IV drug users and unprotected sexual intercourse. Before considering attempts at countering risky behaviours, let me say something about the issue of screening for HIV.

Screening for HIV

As it is possible to test for HIV infection by identifying the antibodies associated with it, a number of forms of population screening have been advocated. It is an advocacy that certainly resonates with much of public opinion.

While a few, smaller countries have proposed mandatory screening for their entire population, the unpracticality of such an approach is immediately apparent. There are simply insufficient resources. Other countries, most noticeably the USA, require testing for immigrants, while many have introduced legislation that requires that particular groups within the population, e.g., IV drug users and prostitutes, be tested. There are a number of problems with even partial screening of this sort. The first concerns the relationship between antibody and virus. Anti-bodies can take variable times to develop following HIV infection, and all a negative result on testing indicates is that an individual is without antibodies at the time of testing. The virus might still be present. What evidence there is suggests that for most people antibodies develop within a few weeks of infection. However, for some there can be some delay. The precise temporal distribution of antibody appearance following likely infection has yet to be fully determined. What can be said, though, is that the evidence indicates variability. Further, an individual may become infected shortly after receiving a negative test outcome. What all of this means is that in order to ensure continuing freedom from infection, continuous tests would have to be administered. Again, we hit the issue of practicality. Two additional problems surround mandatory testing of currently at-risk groups, such as prostitutes and IV drug users. First of all, it may serve to drive such marginal groups further underground, and by purposely making themselves unavailable for testing they also put themselves outside the reach of public health programmes, such as, in the case of IV drug users, those involving clean syringe distribution. Second, screening of high risk groups may encourage the belief among those not in such groups that the spread of AIDS will be effectively countered by these measures, and so serve to enhance illusions of personal invulnerability. In all probability this will reduce the likelihood of preventative behaviours being adopted. Thus, as Phillips and White (1991) cogently argue, 'Long-term reliance on screening to prevent AIDS is a recipe for the increasing prevalence of HIV infection'.

Screening may serve an important function, though, in helping determine more accurately the true incidence of HIV infection in particular communities. In many countries, voluntary HIV testing is available for those who regard themselves as at risk, and many of the estimates of HIV infection and projected AIDS prevalence are based on the outcomes of such tests. However, as implied earlier, estimates based on voluntary testing are likely to be under-estimates. Accordingly, anonymous testing has been undertaken in a number of countries as a means of supplementing the data base and deriving better estimates of infection incidence. Blood samples which are obtained for other reasons, e.g., from pregnant women, from people attending at clinics for sexually transmitted diseases, and from hospital inpatients, are tested for HIV. Obviously, such testing raises ethical issues, particularly of consent. It is generally considered problematic in western countries to expose people to medical procedures without their consent. The requirement for consent is waived only under the most special circumstances. However, it has been argued that AIDS, its rapid spread, and the urgent need to develop effective prevention strategies and to plan care provision constitute very special circumstances indeed. Another issue that surrounds anonymous testing concerns the absence of benefit to the testee. It is likely that some of those tested, e.g., pregnant women, might wish to know their HIV status, if positive. This, in turn, raises a general issue related to screening: what to do about those who have to receive news of a positive HIV test. This is no easy matter. As might be guessed, undergoing a test for HIV antibodies is itself an exceedingly stressful experience. In a recent study Ironson *et al.* (1990) examined changes in immunological functioning in a group of homosexual men who had undergone a test for HIV and were waiting to learn the outcome. Despite the fact that they were ultimately shown to be HIV-negative, they showed reduced immunological reactions to antigen introduction. Indeed, immunological functioning took five weeks following notification of the absence of HIV antibodies to return to normal. In a further report, Antoni *et al.* (1990) reported that plasma cortisol (a hormone responsive to severe psychological stress) levels were substantially elevated in anticipation of the test result and the elevation showed much the same time course as the immune system disruption.

This very much suggests the need for supportive counselling for those undergoing such tests, irrespective of their subsequent HIV status. However, when someone tests positive, there are obviously substantial additional coping demands. Blaney *et al.* (1990) found that asymptomatic, but HIV-positive, homosexual men evidenced more emotional distress and experienced more stressful life events than HIV-negative homosexual control subjects. All too often, though, appropriate support is not always available. Gatchel *et al.* (1989) provide us with an example of what would appear to be a model of good practice in the USA.

Following a positive HIV test, individuals receive thorough psychological evaluation by a social worker, chaplain and psychiatrist; after which they are assigned to a support group which meets at least once a week. The group focuses on the management of grief, depression, feelings of helplessness and fear of dying. In addition, individuals receive an educational programme which provides information on the relationship between stress and immune functioning, the medical and legal aspects of HIV-positive status, stress management, safe sex, and alcohol and drug abuse. Approaches such as these may not only help those who are HIV-positive cope with their status, but may also serve ultimately to reduce the spread of AIDS.

It is not merely a matter of providing support; the tenor of that support is also of importance. Blaney *et al.* (1990) conclude that there is a need for 'accentuating the positive'. That is, it is important, they argue, to convey to infected individuals as well as society at large that HIV infection can be managed effectively, at least for a time. By failing to get this message across, the individual's ability to cope may be further undermined. Several types of research converge to suggest that emphasizing the negative may adversely affect psychological and physical health. This is an extremely important matter in the case of HIV-positive individuals, whose disease-fighting capacity is most probably already compromised as a result of the infection. Thus, support and educational programmes should, it is argued, foster awareness of positive coping potential in the early stages of HIV infection, emphasizing that individuals can get on with most of the business of living, despite their HIV status.

Reducing Risky Behaviour

Virtually all western countries have launched national public education campaigns using newspaper advertisements, leaflets, television and radio to convey information about AIDS, its nature and the behaviours that render people at risk of infection. The underlying assumptions, as is the case in most public health promotion, are that the provision of information and the presumed attendant increase in knowledge will prompt attitudes and consequently behaviour to change. There is substantial evidence that challenges such assumptions, and that the progressions from information to knowledge to attitude shift to behaviour change are complex matters, not inevitable consequences.

Let me illustrate this by briefly considering two early AIDS campaigns, one in the UK, the other in Australia. In 1986, the UK government launched its first information campaign relating to AIDS. It was concerned, quite properly, among other things, to counter much of the misleading information that had until then characterized much of the discussion of AIDS in the popular press. Initially, a whole-page advertisement was placed in every national newspaper, which attempted to outline the facts about AIDS, the HIV virus, its mode of transmission, behaviours that increased risk, and safe sex. Evaluations of this campaign indicated that it was less than completely successful. For example, Sherr (1987) reported that individuals tested on AIDS/HIV knowledge before and after the campaign showed only marginal increases in knowledge, and this occurred mainly as a result of the campaign filling in gaps in knowledge rather than correcting misconceptions. In addition, anxiety about AIDS was high in Sherr's subjects before the campaign and was found to be equally high afterwards. Thus, the campaign had little impact on knowledge and did little to combat anxiety.

Subsequent to that early campaign, television, radio and billboard advertisements have been used to enhance public awareness, and gradually, as Phillips (1988) pointed out, public awareness has increased. It is clear that knowledge of AIDS has increased enormously since the mid-1980s, although it is not clear that this can be attributed either directly or wholly to the public health campaigns. However, as Phillips goes on to emphasize, it would be a grave mistake to believe that increased knowledge will be translated into changes in attitude and, critically, alterations in behaviour. Some groups, most noticeably male homosexuals, have responded to the AIDS threat by changing their behaviour in order to reduce risk. However, this most likely reflects the high early incidence of HIV and AIDS among male homosexuals and is attributable not to the public health education programmes, but to local campaigns and initiatives, and experiences within male homosexual networks and communities. However, caution is warranted even here. McKirnan and Peterson (1989) reported from a survey of over 2,000 homosexual men that while some 80 per cent indicated that they had changed their sexual behaviour, the frequency of monogamous stable relationships among the sample was unchanged from that found sixteen years earlier. In addition, 19 per cent of their current sample reported two or more new sexual partners per month. Nevertheless, there is evidence of behavioural change among male homosexuals.

The same cannot be said for the heterosexual community. For example, in a study of adolescents reported by Phillips and White (1991), 70 per cent reported themselves to be sexually active, although only 15 per cent had actually changed their behaviour as a result of the threat of AIDS. In general terms, people frequently take a very optimistic view of their own personal risk and vulnerability to disease. This would seem to be only too evidently the case among heterosexuals with regard to AIDS and HIV infection. For example, O'Leary *et al.* (1991) found that of nearly 400 sexually active, unmarried New Jersey college students, only 24 per cent reported consistently using condoms. Similarly, in a study of sexually active black American women, Johnson *et al.* (1991) reported high levels of knowledge about AIDS, including the reduction of risk of HIV transmission by using condoms during sexual intercourse. On average, over 90 per cent of the sample correctly answered all the questions in the AIDS quiz. However, their attitudes and behaviour belie that knowledge. The women had fairly negative attitudes towards condoms, and this was particularly so for women who were currently involved sexually with more than one partner. In addition, of the women with multiple sexual partners, only 14 per cent reported regularly insisting on condoms. Thus stimulating awareness and imparting knowledge is one thing; changing attitudes and behaviour is something else.

The campaign launched in 1987 in Australia adopted a very different approach to the essentially information-based strategies preferred in the UK and other European countries such as Sweden, Switzerland and West Germany. Distinctly, the Australian approach initially relied on shock tactics. It began with a television commercial featuring the 'Grim Reaper', a skeletal, death-like figure carrying a scythe who creates havoc in bowling alleys, with bowls aimed with deadly intent at the 'pins' which assume the form of men, women and children. It was presumed that through the agency of fear, people would adopt less risky behaviours. Again, however, the impact of messages, including health messages, is not a simple function of their fearfulness. Individuals who are overly frightened may actually avoid further contact with the fearful message rather than change their behaviour in the desired direction by engaging in health-protecting actions. In an independent evaluation of the 'Grim Reaper' campaign, Rigby *et al.* (1989) found little evidence that the campaign had had the desired effect. Five hundred and twenty-five residents in Adelaide were interviewed shortly after the campaign and their understanding and concern about AIDS compared with those from a similar sample interviewed before the campaign. Although just under 94 per cent of those in the former sample recalled seeing the television advertisement, they did not register any significant increase in person or social concern about AIDS; in fact, among older respondents personal concern had actually decreased. In general, levels of knowledge about AIDS appeared to be unchanged by the campaign. Even among the minority of respondents (29 per cent) who most approved of the campaign, knowledge about AIDS was no greater than that found in other subjects, although this minority did report more personal and social concern about AIDS. Thus, the use of frightening material did not seem to provoke the desired sorts of attitudinal changes, and did not do anything for the populace's understanding of AIDS.

In conclusion, it would appear that the vast increase in AIDS awareness and knowledge has arisen almost in spite of, rather than because of, the early campaigns in many countries. Further, as indicated previously, there is no evidence that these or subsequent public health initiatives have resulted in dramatic changes in behaviour particularly among the heterosexual population. Perhaps public health campaigns in general, and AIDS campaigns in particular, would benefit from being launched from a clearer understanding of individuals' beliefs about health and what is likely to provoke them to adopt less risky behaviours.

The Health Belief Model

The health belief model represents an attempt to characterize the factors that influence the likelihood that an individual will undertake health-related actions. First of all, the model specifies that whether individuals are ready to take such action will depend crucially on their perceptions of the severity of the disease and of their vulnerability to it. Thus, if an individual believes that the disease in question is not serious and does not believe that he or she has much of a chance of contracting the disease, the readiness to act will be low. Second, the model postulates that even when an individual is ready to act, whether or not he or she actually acts depends on an analysis of benefits against costs. If the costs are perceived as great and/or immediate and the benefits as few and/or nebulous and distant, there will be little chance of evasive action being taken. Finally, there must be what is termed a cue to action, either an internal cue (such as bodily symptoms) or an external cue (such as a health campaign). Such cues, in general terms, make the individual aware that something is amiss.

A brief pause to consider this health belief model in the context of HIV/AIDS indicates the difficulties that face those who devise public health campaigns. While there is evidence that populations regard AIDS as a serious disease, more severe, in fact, than any other, many estimate themselves as having low personal risk. It is often the case that individuals are overly optimistic about their own vulnerability to disease, and this is nowhere more apparent at the moment than in people's, particularly heterosexuals', perceptions of their own personal vulnerability to AIDS. This is a clear obstacle to behavioural change. Even where there is readiness to change, the costs may appear to outweigh the perceived benefit in risk reduction. In the studies of condom use cited earlier, many of the subjects indicated that condoms interfered with their enjoyment, or were disliked by their partners. For many, it was evident that such perceived costs of condom use outweighed their estimate of the personal risk reduction benefit that might accrue from using condoms.

However, behavioural change is possible, as evidenced by changes reported in their behaviour by homosexual men. They report marked increases in the use of condoms, and objective evidence of this is reflected in the general overall reduction in the incidence of sexually transmitted diseases such as gonorrhoea among homosexual men in many countries. Effects such as these indicate the importance of smaller communities in encouraging and sponsoring changes in behaviour among their members, and argue that campaigns addressed at heterosexuals may have to be targeted more locally in order to succeed.

As indicated previously, it has been the sharing of contaminated needles that has caused the spread of HIV among IV drug users. This is nowhere better illustrated than in the city of Edinburgh. According to Mulleady (1987), in 1983 blood samples taken from IV drug users in the West Granton area of Edinburgh were among the first in Britain to reveal the presence of HIV. The estimated rate of infection among this group in 1983 was around 3 per cent. Estimates twelve months later suggested a rate of 50 per cent and HIV is now endemic among Edinburgh IV drug users. In Glasgow, just over forty miles away, the rate among IV drug users in 1986 was around 4.5 per cent. Why the difference? Phillips and White (1991) explain. In both cities it is legal for pharmacists to sell syringes to IV drug users. However, in Edinburgh the police have pursued a policy of arresting individuals found with injecting equipment, whereas in Glasgow there was no such policy. In both cities needles were shared, but in Glasgow it occurred in small locally-based groups. In Edinburgh, the police policy has determined that sharing occurs between many more IV drug users, by encouraging the strategy, to reduce the risk of arrest, of injecting using shared 'works' at the point of drug purchase: i.e., drug injection in Edinburgh frequently takes place in so-called shooting galleries where many and diverse individuals share needles. Clearly, policies which reduce the perceived necessity of needle sharing need to be adopted. In addition, accessible facilities for obtaining clean syringes are required, along with making IV drug users aware of the risk of sharing contaminated needles.

There is some evidence, at least in some countries, that these messages are getting home and resulting in behaviour change. For example, in a study reported as early as 1986, Selwyn reported that 84 per cent of the IV drug users interviewed indicated that they would stop sharing syringes if they had access to a steady supply of sterile ones. Mulleady (1987) related that Amsterdam had already established needle exchange units, and since their introduction over 400,000 syringes had been issued, with a return rate of 90 per cent. AIDS in the West is currently increasing more rapidly among IV drug users than among any other group. They also represent the bridge to heterosexual HIV infection. While the initiatives listed above, among others, are important, it may be that higher order policies including the decriminalization of certain aspects of drug use will be necessary in order to bring IV drug users within the ambit of educational provision and community-based projects. It might be countered that approaches such as these will serve simply to encourage higher incidences of IV drug use. There is no evidence that this is the case. However, there is substantial evidence that punitive approaches to drug use in the West have not met with noticeable success.

Concluding Remarks

While the need to persuade people to adopt safe sexual practices and, if they are IV drug users, to abandon needle sharing remains paramount, it is difficult to end this chapter without reconsidering those who have contracted HIV or who have AIDS or ARC. It is clear that virtually all western countries will have to make substantial psychological and medical provision available. I have touched on some of the counselling demands already. Let me return to these briefly.

While the factors that influence the rate of progress of the virus in HIV-positive individuals and account for the marked individual variation in the latency of AIDS following infection remain unclear, a number have been suggested. Among these is psychological stress. As we have already seen, stress can operate to reduce the efficiency of the immune system, and we can speculate that this might be a particular problem for individuals whose immune system is already compromised by HIV infection. It has been clear for some time that the impact of other viruses is affected by stress. For example, Jacobs *et al.* (1969) found a relationship between naturally occurring colds and the incidence of stressful life events. In a more controlled study conducted at the Common Cold Unit in Salisbury, England, by Totman *et al.* (1980), subjects were administered nasal drops containing the cold virus. Symptom appearance was again related to measures of life stress. The implications of such results for the impact of HIV are self-evident, and they also echo a point made earlier that stress management emphasizing positive coping potential should very much be part of any counselling protocol.

Chapter 6

Stress Management: Reducing the Risk of Coronary Heart Disease

Health psychology is concerned not only with the manner in which our behaviour and social circumstances, such as the amount and nature of the stressors we are exposed to, contribute to the development and progress of disease. Far from it. Health psychology is very much a practical project, with the goal of evaluating the application of psychological techniques in the management and, even more ambitiously, in the prevention of disease. The reader hopefully got some flavour of this from the chapter on AIDS, and the discussion of public health strategies for reducing the incidence of high risk behaviours. The remaining chapters of this text will attempt to provide other examples: looking at pain and its management; understanding why people do not always adhere to medical or therapeutic advice; evaluating the value of physical exercise in promoting health, as well as considering the physiological and psychological sequelae of exercise and physical fitness. First of all, though, this chapter will be concerned with the application of psychological techniques to reduce the risk of CHD. I shall focus on one particular technique or set of techniques, generally referred to as stress management training.

Stress Management Training

Stress management training is a generic term of a variety of techniques all aimed at reducing the impact of psychological stress. Among these are: education about the nature of stress and its implications for disease; substantial training and practice in relaxation and/or meditation; stress inoculation, in which individuals are encouraged to redefine stressors and to adopt more positive orientations to stressful situations; the use of imagery to allow people to rehearse coping with frequently encountered stressors in their mind, as preparation for coping with them in real life; schooling in effective coping strategies; cognitive restructuring, in which people are encouraged to rearrange their thinking and reorder their priorities. Not all of these will be present in every therapeutic intervention adorned with the title of stress management training. Conversely, some forms of stress management training may include other specifically focused approaches, such as teaching people to reduce type A behaviour, or getting them to manage anger better. Whatever the precise arrangement and form of stress management training, its goal is to help people cope better with the challenges and stresses of their lives. The underlying presumption is that in doing so the risk of disease onset or recurrence will be ameliorated.

Stress Management Training and CHD

Stress management training has probably been examined most extensively in the area of CHD risk. As indicated earlier, many of the identified risk factors for CHD have a behavioural or psychological component. Type A behaviour and hypertension, discussed earlier, spring readily to mind. In order to illustrate the application of stress management training in this context, discussion will focus on these two CHD risk factors and, in addition, offer a brief consideration of its efficacy in reducing serum cholesterol.

Serum Cholesterol

Levels of serum cholesterol above 5.2 mmol/litre significantly raise an individual's risk of developing CHD. The favoured non-pharmacological approach to reducing high cholesterol levels has, to date, been dietary manipulation. However, the relationship between dietary cholesterol and serum cholesterol levels remains unclear. Nevertheless, most studies of dietary intervention can point to at least some reduction in serum cholesterol as a result of reduced cholesterol intake. Unfortunately, such reductions appear to have very little impact on mortality from CHD. Recently, Muldoon *et al.* (1990) reviewed six key studies which had compared serum cholesterol reduction treatments with either no treatment or a control treatment in terms of the incidence of subsequent CHD-related deaths. Four of the studies involved pharmacological treatments, but two applied dietary interventions. Taken together, the six studies encompassed almost 25,000 participants who, on average, were followed up for almost five years. Overall, the drug or dietary treatments yielded serum cholesterol reductions of around 10 per cent.

The results of the review can, at best, be described as disappointing. While those who had received the cholesterol-reducing treatment had a lower incidence of CHD-related deaths in the follow-up period than the control group subjects, the difference was not statistically reliable. Further, when one examines just the two dietary intervention studies alone, the picture is even less impressive. Of the 164 CHD-related deaths in the two dietary intervention studies, eighty occurred in the treatment groups and eighty-four in the control groups, i.e., the dietary treatment conferred no advantage whatsoever on individuals as far as CHD-related mortality was concerned. The indications for dietary intervention get even bleaker, though, when one considers death from other causes. There were reliably fewer deaths from cancer, as well as deaths from causes not related to illness (accident, suicide) recorded for participants in the control groups in these studies than for subjects in the cholesterol treatment groups. This pattern was true for both pharmacological and dietary intervention. For the two dietary studies, seventeen participants in the dietary treatments had died from cancer by the end of the studies, compared with only twenty-nine of the control group subjects; the analogous figures for death from causes unrelated to illness were twenty-five and fourteen.

These data suggest that to focus exclusively on lowering serum cholesterol, while ignoring other CHD risk factors, may be a rather fruitless activity. They should also serve as a caution to the more strident public advocates of healthy eating programmes where 'healthy' is narrowly defined as low in cholesterol. Radically altering one's diet is not at all an easy matter for many people, particularly those in less favourable material circumstances with little or no choice about where they shop for food. If, in the absence of other changes in life style and material circumstances, there is little benefit to be gained, and, if anything, possible adverse sequelae, remonstrations about diet by politicians, among others, can but be regarded as not only somewhat arrogant but wholly inappropriate.

With regard to the first of these conclusions, it is important to remind the reader that serum cholesterol levels are related to matters other than diet. Two factors are worthy of mention in the current context. There is evidence (see, e.g., Lovallo and Pishkin, 1980) that type A behaviour is associated with raised serum cholesterol. In addition, the incidence of stressful life events also seems to be related to cholesterol level (see, e.g., Francis, 1979). In Chapter 2, I cited results indicating that individuals classified as showing type A behaviour appeared to experience a relatively high incidence of stressful life events. That aside, the findings above suggest that another method of reducing serum cholesterol may be through the use of stress management techniques, i.e., a possible side benefit of applying these techniques to type A behaviour and to hypertension may be a reduction in serum cholesterol.

Let us consider the evidence to date. Roskies *et al.* (1979) provided subjects with either a fourteen-week programme of psychotherapy based on psychoanalytic approaches or a similar duration stress management intervention that emphasized training and practice in relaxation. Serum cholesterol was measured at outset, after treatment, and at six-month follow-up. Immediately after treatment both the psychotherapy and the stress management training were associated with reliable reductions in cholesterol level. However, at six-month follow-up these lower cholesterol levels were maintained only in the stress management subjects. It is important to emphasize that subjects were required not to alter their diets during the study, and thus it is difficult to attribute serum cholesterol reductions here to dietary change. Similar findings emerge from an earlier study by Suinn (1975). Patients, following myocardial infarction, were allocated to either stress management training or to a no-treatment control condition. Five sessions of stress management training were provided. Again patients were urged not to alter their diets. Following training, patients registered significant reductions in cholesterol level. No such reductions were observed for the no-treatment group. Finally, Cooper (1982) examined the impact of a meditation-based stress management programme on subjects with high levels of serum cholesterol. After excluding subjects who had radically changed their diet during the course of the study, the twelve subjects who had undergone stress management training evidenced, on average, a substantial reduction in serum cholesterol at one-year follow-up. No such changes were seen in eleven control subjects. Although not all studies have found such an effect (see, e.g., Patel *et al.*, 1985), the broad thrust of the evidence to date is that stress management training would seem to be a useful vehicle for achieving reductions in serum cholesterol.

Type A Behaviour

While a number of small-scale studies have shown that stress management training can be effective in reducing type A behaviour (e.g., Suinn and Bloom, 1978), the most impressive evidence to date that type A behaviour is modifiable and that its modification has implications for CHD comes from the Recurrent Coronary Prevention Project. The final report on the project was presented by Friedman *et al.* in 1986. This was a massive-scale project, with important implications, so it is perhaps worth devoting a little time to describing it in some detail.

At the outset, over a thousand subjects who had either one or more documented myocardial infarction six months or more earlier were recruited. Subjects were 64 years old or younger, none currently smoked, 90 per cent were men, and the vast majority were white. Most were from the San Francisco area. Eight hundred and sixty-two of those recruited agreed to be randomly allocated to either a control group, which received routine cardiac counselling, focused on medication, diet, and exercise advice, but did not include a discussion of stress-related behaviour, or to a condition in which routine counselling was augmented with a stress management programme. The core of this programme was the goal of developing an awareness of type A behaviour, its manifestations and health consequences. A wide variety of techniques were used to this end. They included relaxation, cognitive restructuring and behavioural contracting, where specific agreed tasks were assigned aimed at changing emotional and behavioural reactions to stress. Two hundred and seventy participants were allocated to the routine cardiac counselling condition, 592 to the counselling plus stress management condition. Both counselling and counselling plus stress management were provided in a small group context. The small groups met at increasing intervals for the four-and-a-half-year life of the project. The remaining 151 patients did not receive group counselling of any kind. Assessments were made yearly for the first three years and at the end of the project, i.e., at four and a half years. At virtually all stages in the project the individuals receiving stress management plus cardiac counselling treatment faired better in terms of cumulative reinfarction rate than the group receiving only cardiac counselling. By the final assessment, some 35 per cent of the stress management subjects evidenced a marked reduction in type A behaviour, assessed by questionnaire, videotaped structured interview, and the testimony of a spouse or other intimate. In contrast, under 10 per cent of the cardiac-counselling-alone subjects showed a reduction in type A behaviour. With regard to recurrence of myocardial infarction, the cumulative four-and-a-half-year incidence was 12.9 per cent for the stress management training group, but almost double that, at 21.2 per cent, for the cardiac counselling group. The comparison group, not receiving any sort of formal intervention, registered a recurrence rate of 28.2 per cent. Finally, participants in either of the two intervention groups who reported substantial reductions in type A behaviour by the end of the first year of study had significantly fewer recurrences of myocardial infarction in the remaining three and a half years than those who reported little or no change. These data are indeed persuasive, and indicate that where type A behaviour is a predominant characteristic (a staggering 95 per cent of participants showed type A behaviour at the outset of the study), stress management training aimed at altering type A behaviour can be successful in achieving changes in the desired direction, and that such changes are associated with manifest benefits in terms of CHD recurrence. However, as I indicated earlier, type A behaviour may be particularly prevalent in some populations and cultures; elsewhere, though, other risk factors may predominate. One of the possible advantages of stress management training is that it may be beneficial across a number of risk factors. We have already considered the evidence that it can effect reductions in serum cholesterol, although it should be pointed out that sizeable reductions in cholesterol level were apparent in both the treatment groups in the Recurrent Coronary Prevention Project (16.3 per cent in the cardiac counselling group and 18.6 per cent in the stress management plus cardiac counselling group), and are, accordingly, probably attributable in this instance mainly to changes in diet.

Hypertension

Of all CHD risk factors, most attention, in terms of stress management, has been directed at hypertension. While pharmacological treatment of hypertension has been successful in dramatically reducing the incidence of stroke (Pooling Project Research Group, 1978), the evidence for CHD is much more mixed. Although there have been successes, there have also been studies reporting only slight or marginal reductions in CHD events (e.g., Medical Research Council Working Party, 1985). In addition, anti-hypertensive medication is often associated with side effects. These, as well as other factors, undoubtedly underlie the high levels of non-adherence to prescriptions. Considerations of this sort have prompted the search for alternative, non-pharmacological approaches to treatment. Earliest among these was biofeedback (see, e.g., Carroll, 1984). Briefly, hypertensive individuals were given regular visual or auditory feedback of their blood pressure. Armed with such feedback it was presumed that hypertensive individuals would be able, through voluntary control, to effect reductions in their blood pressure. A number of studies in the 1970s were conducted to examine the efficacy of biofeedback as a means of combating hypertension. Considered overall, however, they offer neither consistent nor unambiguous support for the application of biofeedback to high blood pressure. while most bear witness to some reductions in blood pressure, a significant number report only marginal effects or none at all. In addition, many of the studies are compromised by methodological weaknesses. For example, only a handful of studies included any follow-up assessment. Of these, hardly any reveal sustained reductions in blood pressure.

An exception to this generally disappointing picture are the results of the studies conducted by Patel and her associates. However, the effects observed in these studies can hardly be attributed to biofeedback. While Patel did use biofeedback, it was feedback of skin electrical resistance or muscle tension that was provided, and not blood pressure. Further, biofeedback was given as an aid to relaxation, and imbedded in a complex package of treatments, which had relaxation, meditation and other elements of stress management as their core. Accordingly, this research is best viewed as a test of the efficacy of stress management training in achieving reductions in blood pressure.

Let me summarize the outcome of this research. The treatment developed by Patel and her colleagues consists of a flexible combination of progressive muscular relaxation, meditation, breathing exercises from yoga, biofeedback to encourage increases in the skin's electrical resistance (since the skin resistance of the hands decreases sharply under conditions of stress, an increase in resistance can be regarded as a shift towards a less aroused, more relaxed state) or for reductions in muscle tension, and training in the self-management of stress. These are supplemented by employing a variety of media to get across to patients the relationship between stress and hypertension.

In the first of two controlled studies (Patel, 1975), forty hypertensives were allocated in equal numbers either to the above stress management programme or to a simple control procedure. The stress management training continued for three months with approximately three sessions per week. Patients in the control condition attended for the same amount of time but merely rested quietly. The results were clear cut; while the blood pressure of patients in the control condition remained unchanged throughout the study, dramatic reductions were evident for the stress management group. On average, pressure for this group fell from an initial baseline of 159/100 mm Hg to 139/86 mm Hg by the end of training. Assessment at three, six, nine and twelve months following indicated these gains had been maintained. In addition, the levels of anti-hypertensive medication were able to be reduced substantially for twelve of the twenty stress management patients, and they were still on reduced drug dosages at the twelve-month follow-up.

Patel and North (1975) found much the same sort of effect, but with less extensive training. Thirty-four hypertensive patients took part in this study and were again assigned either to the stress management condition already described or to a control condition which consisted of resting quietly and having their blood pressures measured. Each group of patients in this study received twelve sessions of their allocated treatment. Whereas blood pressure fell impressively for the stress management patients by 26 mm Hg, systolic, and 15 mm Hg, diastolic, the control group patients showed much less spectacular reductions: 9 mm Hg and 5 mm Hg, systolic and diastolic respectively.

Assessment three months after the termination of formal treatment indicated that while blood pressure had risen slightly for the stress management group (from 141/84 to 149/88 mm Hg), it was still strikingly lower than at entry to the study, and had drifted upward less than was the case for the control group (from 160/99 to 177/104 mm Hg). It was also possible, as in the earlier study, to reduce the medication dosage levels of some of the stress management patients. Finally, at the end of this study, the control group patients received twelve sessions of the stress management package. Although their blood pressure had changed only slightly during the previous resting quietly and blood pressure assessment condition, these patients now registered maked reductions in blood pressure. Systolic blood pressure fell on average by 28 mm Hg and diastolic pressure by 15 mm Hg.

Since most of the patients in these two studies were on some kind of anti-hypertensive medication, it is always possible in such circumstances that the stress management treatment worked mainly because it increased adherence to medication, i.e., it increased the regularity with which patients took their prescribed anti-hypertensive drugs. While the fact that drug dosage levels were able to be reduced for some patients receiving stress management training argues against such an interpretation, it does not completely counter it.

Consequently, it is important to establish these effects in unmedicated hypertensive patients. In this context, the study conducted by Patel *et al.* (1981) is important in that it was both a large-scale study and one which used non-medicated hypertensives, selected from workers at a factory on the basis of a blood pressure screening programme. Almost 200 men entered the study, but data are reported on fifty of them who underwent the stress management treatment and a further forty-three who served as no-treatment control subjects. For the treatment group, systolic blood pressure fell by 20 mm Hg on average, and diastolic blood pressure by 11 mm Hg, and these gains were maintained at six-month follow up. The no-treatment group showed blood pressure reductions less that half this magnitude (11 mm Hg and 4 mm Hg respectively for systolic and diastolic pressure). By the four-year follow-up (Patel *et al.*, 1985), while neither systolic nor diastolic pressures were as low as immediately post-treatment, the pressures recorded for the stress management group remained below the levels recorded at entry to the study, and were significantly lower than control group levels.

I have devoted a fair deal of space to the research of Patel and her colleagues. Rightly so, I would contend, since it represents a concerted programme, where all studies point in the same general direction; stress management can be an effective force for lowering blood pressure. Nevertheless, confirmation of this by other researchers would be no bad thing. Fortunately, there are now a number of independent studies, which, while not reporting quite such impressive gains as Patel, do confirm that stress management training can effect reductions in blood pressure. Two examples may serve to illustrate.

Irvine *et al.* (1986) compared a stress management programme similar to that of Patel with an ingenious placebo control condition, which consisted of mobility and flexibility exercises which subjects were led to believe would lower peripheral resistance by helping dilate blood vessels, and hence reduce blood pressure; there was no mention of stress or its control in this condition. Following treatment, blood pressure in the stress management group dropped significantly by 6 mm Hg systolic and 5 mm Hg diastolic, whereas for the placebo flexing group, blood pressure had actually increased during the same period by 0.5 mm Hg systolic and by 4.5 mm Hg diastolic. The picture at three-month follow-up was very much the same. The results reported above are for unmedicated subjects only; subjects on anti-hypertensive medication, though, showed similar changes.

Finally, Agras *et al.* (1983) exposed eight hypertensives to an eight-week stress management programme. A novel feature of this study is that pressures were not only monitored in the clinic, but also every twenty minutes throughout the working day by means of semi-automatic blood pressure monitors. Immediately after treatment, pressures measured at the clinic showed substantial reductions (14 and 13 mm Hg for systolic and diastolic pressure respectively). So, did pressures at the worksite (8 and 6 mm Hg respectively). These effects were still, to a substantial extent, visible at follow-up, one year after the termination of the study.

Stress Management Training and Multiple Risk Factors

The foregoing evidence of benefits regarding serum cholesterol, type A behaviour and hypertension suggests that stress management techniques might prove an effective intervention for individuals who possess multiple risk factors. In fact, it can be argued that stress management's greatest potential is its applicability to a variety of risk factors.

In the context of CHD, this is an important matter. Risk factors for heart disease operate in a multiplicative, not an additive, fashion, i.e., the possession of two risk factors confers four times, rather than double, the risk that one risk factor brings. Thus, risk factor intervention should ideally target as many identified risk factors as possible, preferably using the minimum number and variety of interventions. Further, reducing the level of a number of risk factors using a generalized intervention, such as stress management, may be more powerful in terms of risk reduction than reducing only one risk factor, even if each risk factor is not reduced optimally.

Only one study so far that I am aware of has applied stress management techniques to individuals possessing more than one risk factor, with the prime purpose of examining whether stress management can effect changes in different risk factors simultaneously. Accordingly, it is perhaps worth considering this study in some detail.

Bennett *et al.* (1991) selected hypertension and type A behaviour as the two risk factors which, on the basis of previous evidence, were mostly likely to benefit from a stress management intervention. Forty-four unmedicated hypertensive middle-aged men, revealed as showing type A behaviour in the structured interview assessment, were randomly allocated to one of three conditions: stress management training, type A management training, or delayed type A management training. The stress management training involved eight two-hour weekly intervention sessions during which participants met in small groups with the therapist. The first session involved education on the nature of blood pressure, the role of stress in its development, and the beginning of training in relaxation techniques. The second and third sessions involved training in self-instruction and cognitive restructuring, while the fourth session comprised training in simple meditation techniques. In the final four sessions participants practised all of these techniques, took part in role playing and group problem-solving tasks. In all, fifteen participants undertook this stress management programme. A further fifteen participated in the type A management programme, which was identical to the stress management schedule for the first four sessions. In the fifth and sixth sessions, however, participants in type A management training received instruction about time-urgent behaviour and training in time management. The seventh session was given over to improving the control of anger and the final session involved brief training in assertiveness. Blood pressure at rest and during the challenge of the structured interview, and various measures of type A behaviour, were taken at the outset of the study following treatment, and at follow-up six months later. The third group, comprising fourteen participants, had blood pressure and type A behaviour assessed before and after an eight-week period of minimal intervention, following which they received the type A management programme, and were reassessed at the end of the eight-week treatment. In the former two groups, resting blood pressure dropped reliably following treatment. In the stress management group the reduction was from 156/93 to 148/85 mm Hg; the analogous figures for the type A management group were 149/93 and 140/86 mm Hg. These reductions were maintained at follow-up six months later; for the stress management group blood pressure at follow-up averaged 146/88 mm Hg and for the type A management group 137/87 mm Hg. For the delayed intervention group, blood pressure did not change over the eight weeks of minimal intervention. At the outset it was 151/94 mm Hg on average, and eight weeks later it was 153/95 mm Hg. However, with the provision of type A management training to this group, a reliable drop in blood pressure was recorded; after the eight weeks of the programme resting pressure was 142/88 mm Hg. Parallel effects were found for type A behaviour, whether assessed by questionnaire or by structured interview. While the type A management programme was more successful in changing some type A behaviours, such as anger and hostility, stress management training still effected reliable changes in overall questionnaire-assessed type A behaviour, and these gains were maintained at follow-up. The authors draw two major conclusions from the study. First of all, it would seem that it is possible to modify two CHD risk factors, hypertension and type A behaviour, simultaneously, using psychological techniques. Second, while both the stress management and type A behaviour management programmes reduced blood pressure equally well, the type A behaviour intervention was superior in modifying key aspects of type A behaviour, particularly anger and hostility.

The weakness of this study was its rather brief nature; it would have proved instructive to determine what long-term benefits for CHD accrued from such risk factor modification. One recent study which has attempted such a determination is the Lifestyle Heart Trial (Ornish *et al.*, 1990). Twenty-eight patients with coronary atherosclerosis were assigned to a life style management programme, in which they were prescribed stress management training, a low-fat vegetarian diet, and moderate exercise. A further twenty patients were assigned to a control 'usual-care' condition, in which there was no instruction or assistance given to change lifestyle. A variety of problems reduced the effective sample to twenty-two in the life style intervention group and to nineteen in the control group. Assessments of blood pressure, serum cholesterol, and adherence to the life style programme, as well as objective measurements of the degree of atherosclerosis and subjective symptoms of angina, were made at the outset and again twelve months later. During the year, subjects in the life-style management programme had shown high levels of adherence to their new life style regimens. In addition, serum cholesterol levels dropped substantially in the life style management group; there were no such reductions in the control group. Weight also decreased in the life style management group. While blood pressure was little altered in these subjects, most were normotensive on entry to the study. Finally, while both atherosclerosis and angina symptomatology showed signs of improvement in the life style management group, further deterioration characterized the control group participants. Although this study is small-scale, it does indicate that individuals can undertake and sustain quite radical life style modifications, and that such modifications would appear to have implications for the progress of CHD.

Concluding Remarks

In this chapter we have examined the role of behavioural change, in particular that afforded by stress management or related type A behaviour management techniques, in reducing CHD risk. The evidence to date suggests that such techniques can be effective in modifying risk and, which is perhaps even more encouraging, that psychological approaches to managing behaviour and life style can affect a number of risk factors simultaneously. I have a strong feeling that this is where the future lies. However, it is probably worth ending with something of a caveat.

Health psychologists and others should be careful not to overemphasize at this stage the benefits to be gained from life style management. After all, individual life style factors (diet, smoking, exercise, type A behaviour, etc.) are not the only correlates of CHD. Material well-being is also powerfully predictive (Davey Smith *et al.*, 1990). This is a matter I have already alluded to in Chapter 2. While some have presumed to reduce sociodemographic and material influences to matters of individual behaviour and life style (e.g., Matthews, 1989a), they continue to defy such reductionism. CHD still predominates in most western countries, and in the UK particularly, among the lower social classes. As social disparities in income and material benefit increase as they have done in recent years in the UK, so too do the inequalities in health and disease, including CHD. Accordingly, we should be careful not to treat CHD as entirely, or even in the main, dependent on individual behaviour, and, as a consequence, exclusively promote individual prescriptions that emphasize life style and behaviour change. While the sorts of remedies discussed in this chapter are almost certainly effective and useful, they can only ever address part of the problem. I strongly suspect that until we address the gross social and material inequalities in our society we shall continue to suffer from an epidemic of CHD.

Chapter 7

Exercise, Fitness, and Health

In the previous chapter I mentioned the recent research of Ornish and his associates which seemed to indicate that changes in life style can yield positive benefits for health, retarding the progress of coronary heart disease. Part of the complex programme undertaken by patients in this study was physical exercise. While few details are provided about the nature of the exercise, patients were asked to exercise for a minimum of three hours per week and to spend a minimum of thirty minutes per session exercising within targets set on the basis of their heart rates during a treadmill test. Ornish *et al.* describe their prescription as moderate, aerobic exercise, and typically it was walking.

Moderate exercise is now a common prescription for CHD patients, and the available evidence indicates that it has beneficial effects. For example, CHD patients undertaking exercise have been observed to gain earlier release from hospital, to achieve more complete return to work, and to evidence increased survival rates (see, e.g., Wenger, 1978, 1979). However, it has also been observed that CHD patients often show poor compliance with the prescribed exercise regimes. General issues of compliance with therapy will be addressed in the next chapter.

At the same time, it has been argued that exercise can be highly effective in primary prevention for CHD, i.e., that habitual physical exercise may reduce the risk of CHD in the first place. There is certainly a fair deal of epidemiological evidence to indicate that exercise may be a good bet. Before considering that, let me briefly say what is meant by exercise in this context.

In general, researchers are referring to aerobic exercise of sufficient intensity to produce stable physiological benefits. Aerobic exercise comprises exertions such as walking, running and swimming in which oxygen uptake and heart rate are increased in order to facilitate the extra physical work undertaken. In essence, it is endurance exercise. Among the physiological benefits are lower resting heart rate and increased vital capacity, i.e., the maximum uptake of oxygen the individual is capable of. The latter is frequently taken as a measure of aerobic fitness. In order to achieve such effects, it is generally agreed that exercise has to be sufficiently vigorous to increase heart rate to at least 60 to 65 per cent of an individual's maximum heart rate, sustained for at least fifteen to thirty minutes, and that such exercise should be undertaken at least three times per week. In contrast, exertions, such as weight-lifting, which require little in the way of sustained increases in oxygen uptake, are generally referred to as anaerobic. Here the increased physical demand is met by mobilizing stored energy resources. In general terms, anaerobic exercises are those concerned with strength rather than endurance.

A Link between Exercise and CHD

Two classic studies are generally cited to illustrate an association between exercise and physical activity on the one hand and CHD on the other, one conducted in the United States, the other in the United Kingdom.

The first, reported in 1977 by Paffenbarger *et al.* examined the work activity and CHD records of San Francisco longshoremen for the years 1951–72. Energy output calculations were made for the various tasks undertaken by the longshoremen, and estimates of average energy expenditure per week ascribed to each of the subjects on the basis of the tasks that they undertook. Subjects were then divided into relatively high and relatively low physical exertion categories, and this categorization compared with CHD mortality during the twenty-two year period, over which time around 11 per cent of the sample had died of CHD. The results were striking. Men in the relatively high physical exertion category had significantly less risk of fatal CHD than men whose job required less exercise. In the case of sudden death (i.e., dead within one hour of a heart attack or on arrival at hospital), the high exertion workers registered only a third of the incidence shown by the low exertion workers. In addition, the effect was evident at any age, but was proportionally strongest for younger men.

The other study focused on leisure time exercise in a group of people in largely sedentary occupations. Morris *et al.* (1980) surveyed the leisure exercise habits of British civil servants by means of a two-day diary report form. On a Monday morning, without advance notice, subjects were asked to describe their activity during the preceding Friday (a work day) and Saturday (a non-work day). The results of the study were based on the analysis of three and a half thousand of these diary reports. The original assessments took place between 1968 and 1970, and the health records of the subjects were then scrutinized for a subsequent period of eight and a half years. The findings were clear cut. Among subjects active in vigorous exercise, there was less than half the incidence of CHD during the follow-up period than there was for the less active subjects. This was true for all indications of CHD: first clinical episode of CHD, first fatal heart attack, and sudden death. In addition, Morris *et al.* found that the rise in CHD mortality with age was strikingly less among the subjects who reported vigorous exercise.

The Protective Effect of Exercise

These data very strongly suggest that exercise exerts a protective effect with regard to CHD. However, the precise mechanisms of that effect remain unclear. A number of possibilities have been mooted. For example, it has been suggested that since the primary cause of CHD is reduced oxygen supply to the muscles of the heart, the most direct benefit of exercise may be to increase the myocardial oxygen supply at rest and/or during periods of increased myocardial oxygen demand, i.e., exercise facilitates a general improvement in the efficiency with which oxygen is delivered to the heart muscle. Alternatively, the aerobic fitness that follows from endurance exercise significantly reduces the heart muscles' demand for oxygen, i.e., by exercising, we are conditioning and strengthening the heart muscle, such that it becomes more efficient. The fit heart, then, will be capable of meeting the same demands as the unfit heart at reduced cost in terms of myocardial energy requirements.

More recently, it has been hypothesized that, in addition to these sorts of mechanisms, exercise training and aerobic fitness may exert an effect by altering the way in which we respond to stress. Physical fitness and exercise, it has been suggested, may afford us protection against the effects of psychological stress. As indicated in the opening chapter of this text, it is clear that a number of factors appear to moderate the relationship between stress on the one hand and disease on the other. A number of researchers have recently suggested that physical fitness may fulfil such a buffering role, although there is little agreement as to how this might happen. One possibility, which arises from the foregoing discussion, is that fitness permits the heart to withstand the activating and disruptive effects of psychological stress more effectively. This, in turn, raises the possibility that fitness alters the manner in which the cardiovascular system in general and the heart in particular respond to stress. A number of studies have now been undertaken to test this proposition.

Fitness and Cardiovascular Reactions to Stress

Two sorts of study have examined the relationship between fitness and exercise and cardiovascular reactions to stress. First of all, a number of studies have compared the reactions of subjects who differ in aerobic fitness or in their conventional levels of physical exercise. Second, a few recent studies have adopted a more interventionist strategy, examining the stress reactions of subjects before and after exposure to an aerobic training programme. Let us consider these in turn.

While counter-examples exist, there is now a reasonably consistent body of evidence to indicate that aerobically fit subjects demonstrate less cardiovascular disruption in the face of psychological stress than unfit subjects. Two examples will serve to illustrate.

Turner *et al.* (1988) recorded heart rate, blood pressure and oxygen consumption while twenty-four healthy young males were exposed to two psychological stressors, a video game and challenging arithmetic (see Chapter 3) and undertook graded exercise on a bicycle. Fitness was assessed by estimating maximum oxygen uptake from values obtained during the bicycle exercise and subjects categorized as either of high or low (in truth, less high) aerobic fitness. Subjects so classified were then compared with regard to activity during the psychological stressors. While the groups registered similar magnitude oxygen consumption values during stress, heart rate was reliably lower for the highly fit subjects. Heart rate reaction to stress was then computed as 'additional' heart rate (see Chapter 3 for a full description of the rationale and computation of 'additional' heart rate). Briefly, for each subject heart rate was plotted against oxygen consumption over the various workloads of the graded exercise task. These regressions were then used in conjunction with the oxygen consumption values during the psychological challenges to predict the expected heart rate values during psychological stress. As has been found previously, the predicted values were significantly lower than the actual heart rate values recorded during psychological stress. However, the discrepancy between predicted and actual values, i.e., 'additional' heart rate, were greater for the less fit subjects. Whereas the average 'additional' heart rate values for the less fit subjects were 14 and 13 beats per minute during the mental arithmetic and video game stressors respectively, the analogous values for the highly fit subjects were 7 and 4 beats per minute respectively.

Light *et al.* (1987) divided their subject sample (174 young healthy men) into thirds on the basis of their self-reported levels of aerobic exercise undertaken weekly. The three groups so constructed were designated as high, medium and low in terms of aerobic exercise. The main active psychological stressor in this study was a shock avoidance reaction time task, in which subjects were threatened that they might receive an electric shock if their reaction times to an intermittent signal were slower than an unquantified criterion. Heart rate, blood pressure and the pre-ejection period of the heart were monitored at baseline and during exposure to the stressor. The latter is a measure thought to reflect the extent of beta-adenergic cardiac activation. The low exercising subjects showed the largest cardiovascular response in terms of heart rate, systolic blood pressure and pre-ejection period, and the high exercising subjects registered the smallest reactions; the moderate group fell in between. Group differences persisted even when group variations at baseline were taken into account.

Studies which have opted for interventionist designs, have been decidedly less successful in demonstrating aerobic training effects on cardiovascular reactions to stress. For example, Sinyor *et al.* (1986) allocated thirty-eight young men to either an aerobic (mainly jogging) or anaerobic (weight-lifting) training group or to a waiting list control group. The training groups met three to four times a week for one hour sessions aimed at either improving aerobic fitness in one case or muscular strength in the other. The training continued for ten weeks, and subjects had their heart rate reactions to a psychological stress measured prior to and following training. Although post-training aerobic fitness measured by estimating maximum oxygen uptake confirmed the effectiveness of the aerobic training programme, no group differences were observed in heart rate reaction to stress.

Two more recent studies (Steptoe *et al.*, 1990; de Geus *et al.*, 1990) also failed to find any noteworthy effects of fitness training on cardiovascular reactions to psychological stress. Steptoe *et al.* allocated seventy-five healthy adults to one of four conditions: a high intensity aerobic training programme, a moderate intensity programme, an undemanding flexibility programme, and a waiting list condition. The training programme lasted ten weeks and subjects' aerobic fitness and cardiovascular reaction to problem-solving stressors were measured before and following completion of the programmes. Although both aerobic training programmes engendered increases in fitness, neither were associated with changes in cardiovascular reactions to the problem-solving stressors. De Geus *et al.* had fourteen young men allocated to a fairly intensive aerobic training programme. These subjects met four times a week for a training session lasting one and a half hours; the programme continued for seven weeks. Eight further subjects put on a waiting list for the programme acted as controls. Cardiovascular reactions to a range of psychological stressors were monitored before and after the seven-week period. Again, the subjects who underwent training showed significant improvements in aerobic fitness. However, none of the indices of cardiovascular reactivity to stress monitored was noticeably affected by training and the associated gains in fitness.

Only two studies, to date, have found reductions in cardiovascular reactions to stress following aerobic training. In one the effect was evident only in a small subsample of borderline hypertensive individuals (Sherwood *et al.*, 1989). In the other, the effects were very marginal (Blumenthal *et al.*, 1988).

It is difficult to know what to make of the lack of consistency of results in this area. Perhaps, given the variety of psychological stress tasks employed in these studies, the frequently small subject samples, and the various and often indirect methods used to assess aerobic fitness, the absence of a clear consensus in terms of outcome is not surprising. However, explanations in terms of methodological factors such as these can hardly explain the results of the studies conducted by Steptoe *et al.* and de Geus *et al.* that I have just mentioned. In addition to examining the effects of aerobic training programmes on reactivity to psychological stress, both of these studies also examined the relationship between the level of aerobic fitness at entry to the study and pre-training physiological reactions to stress. Both observed that more fit subjects tended to show less in the way of physiological disruption in the face of psychological stress.

One possible explanation for the discrepancy in results between cross-sectional analysis and analysis of the effects of training intervention is that individual constitutional differences could be related to both aerobic fitness and cardio-vascular reactivity. Both aerobic fitness and, as we have seen earlier, cardiac reactivity to stress have a substantial genetic component. It is possible that similar gene systems contribute to both fitness and reactivity. If this is the case, we would not expect alterations in fitness with training to be associated with alterations in reactivity. As Steptoe *et al.* pointed out, the implications of such a conclusion are important. It certainly suggests that the protective advantage that exercising and physical activity appears to confer with regard to CHD cannot be mediated by changes in cardiovascular reactions to stress. That component of fitness that derives from intrinsic constitutional factors, in as much as it is important in CHD, may still exert an influence through its co-variation with cardiovascular reactivity to stress. However, the impact on

CHD that derives from the moderation of intrinsic fitness via activity and exercise operates via mechanisms other than the cardiovascular reactivity to stress.

One other possibility is that exercise affects our psychological orientation towards life's stresses and our manner of coping, i.e., perhaps the effects of exercise operate more at a psychological than at a psychophysiological level.

Fitness and the Psychological Impact of Stress

It is certainly the case that several popular publications have been far from reticent in proclaiming the psychological benefits of exercise and fitness, and some exercise and sports participants offer frequent and forceful testimony of their high levels of psychological well-being. However, an early, more detached, academic assessment of the evidence was much more cautious in its conclusions (Folkins and Sime, 1981). In addition, it is surprising just how few objective investigations have been conducted.

Exceptions here are the recent studies conducted by Andrew Steptoe and his colleagues in London and those undertaken by Rick Norris and his associates at the University of Birmingham. Let us briefly consider this research, for while some inconsistencies emerge, it offers a broadly positive picture; regular periods of exercise, and in particular, aerobic training programmes, do seem to afford a range of psychological benefits.

Psychological Benefits of Exercise

Steptoe *et al.* (1989) allocated forty-seven adults who reported relatively high levels of tension and anxiety to one of two conditions: a moderate aerobic training programme, based around walking and jogging, and a flexibility training, designed not to produce increases in aerobic fitness. In both cases training consisted of one supervised and three unsupervised sessions per week. The programmes continued for ten weeks. The drop-out rate was around 30 per cent. Those remaining were assessed post-training using the same measures that were administered pre-training, namely measures of self-reported mood, and questionnaire assessments of anxiety and perceived ability to cope with stress. Fitness was also measured before and after training by means of estimating maximum oxygen uptake from responses on a bicycle exercise machine, and via a twelve-minute run test, where the maximum distance participants could manage to cover in twelve minutes was monitored. The aerobic training programme realized significant improvements in fitness as gauged by both measures. No such improvement was demonstrated by participants in the flexibility programme. In addition, the moderate aerobic exercise programme was associated with reductions in tension and anxiety, decreases in depression, and increases in perceived ability to cope with stress. These gains were still evident at follow-up assessment three months later. The flexibility group appeared to derive little psychological benefit. Thus, while aerobic exercise training may not engender substantial blunting of the cardiovascular reaction to stress, it does seem to have implications for mood and the capacity to cope with stress psychologically.

Confirmation of these effects were reported in a subsequent larger-scale experiment by Moses *et al.* (1989). Here, 109 sedentary adult volunteers were assigned to one of four conditions: high intensity aerobic training (mainly jogging), a moderate intensity exercise programme, as before, the flexibility programme and a waiting list control procedure. As before, the programmes were undertaken for ten weeks, and participants were assessed in terms of mood, anxiety, and coping ability, before and after training, and again at follow-up three months later. Fitness was also assessed at those times by means of the twelve-minute test, and improvements in fitness were largely in line with expectations, with the aerobic training groups deriving most benefit, and the intense aerobic training producing the most marked increases in fitness. Consistent with these researchers' previous results, reductions in anxiety and improvements in perceived coping emerged at post-training and follow-up assessment for the moderate aerobic training group, in contrast to the absence of benefits observed in the flexibility training subjects and those on the waiting list. However, no such effects were evident with high intensity aerobic training. The researchers argue, in interpreting these results, that the superiority observed with moderate exercise may derive from it being more enjoyable, allowing participants to achieve goals of physical activity without exerting undue effort. In contrast, participants in the intense exercise condition may have found training overly demanding, such that any positive benefits in terms of well-being were nullified by the aversiveness of the exercise schedule. This would seem to suggest that it is not just improvements in aerobic fitness that underlie positive psychological effects. The character and context of the exercise may also be of importance.

This idea gets support from the results obtained in the first of two studies recently reported by Norris *et al.* (1990). The participants in this study were police officers from the West Midlands who were assigned to either an aerobic (jogging) or anaerobic (weight-lifting) training group or to a no-treatment control condition. Around twenty-five officers completed each of the two training programmes, which lasted ten weeks and consisted of three sessions per week, two of which were supervised. Fitness was assessed before and after the ten-week period for all three groups by means of measuring the time taken to complete a distance of one and a half miles. In addition, before and after assessments of physical and mental well-being, stress experienced at work, and stress experience in general life were made by questionnaire. The control group showed no positive change in these various psychological measures over time. In contrast, the aerobic group registered reliable reductions in job stress and life stress with training, and marked improvements in physical and mental well-being. As expected, this group's performance on the timed run improved substantially with training. However, the anaerobic training group also derived benefits, in spite of showing no evidence of improved fitness on the timed run; following training they registered reduced life stress and increased physical and mental well-being. These results reinforce the notion that it is not just improvements in aerobic fitness that are the key, since both aerobic and anaerobic training engendered positive psychological effects. It would appear that the benefits accruing from fitness programmes come from a variety of sources; in addition to improvements in fitness, improved body image, feelings of mastery and effectiveness that derive from the completion of an assigned task, and a variety of group dynamic effects are all possibly exerting an influence here.

In a subsequent study, Norris *et al.* (1992) assigned around 150 adolescents to one of four training conditions; these were by and large the same training conditions employed by Steptoe and his associates, i.e., high intensity aerobic training, moderate intensity training, flexibility training and a no-treatment control condition. Fitness was assessed before and after training, using what is called a step-test. Briefly, subjects are required to step on and off a bench for two minutes at a schedule which involves taking thirty steps per minute. Heart rate is measured at rest prior to the test, at the conclusion of the test and again two minutes later. Greater fitness is indexed by a quicker recovery of heart rate to resting levels following exercise. Assessments were also made of mood, with particular focus on anxiety, hostility and depression, of self-reported health, and of perceived stress levels.

Norris *et al.* undertook both a cross-sectional and a longitudinal analysis. In the former, prior to training, it was revealed that participants who reported greater levels of customary physical activity and exertion reported experiencing less stress and less depression. In addition, those adolescents who reported most stress also demonstrated a strong association between stress levels and anxiety, hostility and depression.

The three training groups met twice a week for between twenty-five and thirty minutes, and training lasted for ten weeks. Comparisons between measures before and after training indicated that the high intensity aerobic training programme produced the most marked improvements in fitness. In addition, only subjects undergoing this programme derived any psychological benefit. They reported significantly less stress following training than subjects in the other three groups. Further, the relationship between stress and anxiety, depression and hostility for the high intensity exercise group was substantially weakened at the end of the training periods. For the remaining subjects, though, this relationship was, if anything, strengthened. Thus, in an adolescent population, it would appear to be relatively high intensity aerobic exercise which produces positive effects on well-being. At first glance, these results seem at odds with those reported by Moses *et al.* Undoubtedly, crucial to the discrepancy here are the populations studied. As indicated, the subjects studied by Moses *et al.* were adults, on average in their late thirties. It is possible that what counts as high intensity exercise (i.e., exercise engineered to produce elevations in heart rate to 70–75 per cent maximum heart rate) for adults represents, both physiologically and psychologically, only moderate exercise as far as adolescents are concerned. Thus, when designing exercise programmes, the age of the subjects, in addition to other factors, must be borne in mind.

Taken together, these studies strongly suggest that exercise can yield benefits for subjective well-being and may alter individuals' perceptions of stress and their ability to cope with it. It has yet to be established, though, that it is by such means that exercise and physical activity offer protection against CHD. Nevertheless, this could be a contributory factor, although it is likely to be just one of many.

Exercise and Blood Pressure

Another possible mechanism whereby exercise may exert an effect is through its influence on blood pressure. There is now evidence that aerobic exercise can reduce blood pressure in individuals with hypertension or borderline hypertension. For example, Dubbert *et al.* (1984) reported two case studies of mild hypertensives subject to aerobic training programmes. For one of these subjects, diastolic blood pressure fell from over 90 mm Hg at the outset to around 70 mm Hg after only one week of exercise and remained low for two more weeks as he continued to exercise. With the cessation of exercise, diastolic blood pressure rose again to pre-exercise levels, but fell again with the resumption of exercise. A similar pattern emerged for the second subject. Although diastolic blood pressure rose during the first two weeks of exercise, this could be attributed to the discontinuation of medication. By three weeks, though, this second subject's diastolic blood pressure fell dramatically, and then remained in the normal range for the rest of the exercise period. Four weeks after he stopped the aerobic programme, diastolic blood pressure had returned once more to the mild hypertensive range. Exercise, then, would seem to commend itself as a clinical intervention for hypertension.

A question remains, though, as to whether exercise is generally beneficial for blood pressure, or whether its effects are restricted to those with blood pressures in the hypertensive range. If exercise has a general hypotensive effect across the whole range of blood pressures, then its case as a primary prevention factor in CHD would undoubtedly be strengthened.

It was with this in mind that Norris *et al.* in the two studies previously reported, monitored subjects' blood pressures before and after their exercise interventions. In the first of the studies, both aerobic and anaerobic exercise programmes were associated with substantial reductions in the blood pressures of the police officers who participated. The no-treatment control subjects showed no such change. For the aerobic training group, blood pressure fell from 131/79 mm Hg to 126/71 mm Hg, and for the anaerobic group, who on average registered blood pressure at outset in the borderline hypertensive range, blood pressure fell from 148/91 mm Hg to 134/88 mm Hg. The comparable figures for the control group were 135/86 mm Hg and 136/88 mm Hg. These data suggest that blood pressures not in the hypertensive range can indeed be modified by exercise, and, in addition, that anaerobic exercise may be just as effective as aerobic exercise.

In the second study, which studied adolescents with blood pressures unambiguously in the normotensive range, exercise again appeared to be an effective hypotensive agent. While the effects were statistically significant only for diastolic pressure, the results for systolic pressure were in the same general direction. For the high intensity aerobic exercise group, blood pressure fell from 135/75 mm Hg at outset to 127/72 mm Hg following training, and, for the moderate intensity group, from 127/85 mm Hg to 116/80 mm Hg. The analogous figures for the flexibility training group were 127/73 mm Hg and 126/75 mm Hg, and 125/77 mm Hg and 126/80 mm Hg for the no-treatment control group. Thus even moderate intensity aerobic exercise, which in this adolescent sample produced no noticeable benefits with regard to psychological status, did appear to effect a reduction in blood pressure.

Concluding Remarks

The available evidence suggests that exercise and activity are factors in CHD. Put simply, exercise appears to offer a protective advantage. However, the mechanisms that underlie this advantage remain unclear. One possibility that has received attention recently is that exercise and physical training blunt the cardiovascular impact of psychological stress. However, the available evidence would not seem to offer much in the way of consistent support for this idea. Rather than altering the psychophysiological effects of stress, though, it may be that exercise and fitness alter our psychological orientation towards it and enhance our coping capacities. Here there is much more support. Finally, exercise may operate by affecting acknowledged CHD risk factors. A likely candidate in this respect is blood pressure. It would certainly appear to be the case that exercise training programmes reduce pressure in those with elevated blood pressure. However, there is also recent evidence that exercise may have a more general hypotensive effect, and that moderate exercise can be just as effective as intensive exercise, and anaerobic just as effective as aerobic. It is certain that the effects of exercise are multi-faceted, and it is likely that the gains as far as CHD are concerned arise from a number of sources. However, these demonstrable influences of exercise on blood pressure and on the psychological impact of life stresses represent a good start in untangling just what the effective mechanisms are.

Chapter 8

Taking One's Medicine: Following Therapeutic Advice

As might be suspected, behaviour in medical and paramedical settings is exceedingly complex. Many factors determine how a person behaves in the context of medical personnel and medical institutions. For example, how an individual will respond to a therapeutic prescription has proved exceedingly difficult to predict. It might seem reasonable to presume that if people actively seek help from a physician they will follow the instructions or advice given. However, this would be a rash presumption and one, as we shall see, not supported by the available evidence. There was some hint of this in the previous chapter, when we discussed exercise and training programmes as prescriptions to reduce CHD risk. The commonly reported statistic is that around 50 per cent of individuals drop out of such programmes, or do not fulfil anything close to their requirements. For example, in the study reported by Norris *et al.* (1990) on the effects of exercise training on stress and well-being in West Midlands police officers, fifty volunteer subjects were allocated to either the aerobic or anaerobic training programmes. As the reader will recall, these were ten-week programmes in which subjects were required to undertake three sessions of exercise per week. The main incentives for participation were the opportunity to improve fitness, the regular provision of feedback about progress, and general advice about fitness. However, twenty-eight of the fifty subjects in the aerobic training group completed the programme, and only twenty-four of the anaerobic training group. These proportions are fairly typical.

The issue of what has been termed medical or therapeutic compliance has attracted a substantial amount of attention over the last decade or so. Prior to 1960 the cumulative bibliography on the subject listed only twenty-two articles in English, with 850 being published by 1978. However, more than 3,200 articles in English were listed for the years 1979 to 1985, with more than 1,100 appearing in the years 1984 and 1985 (Trostle, 1988). Nevertheless, even if the research focus is of recent vintage, the problem of people failing to conform to advice or instructions is hardly new. Haynes (1979), in the introduction to a text on the subject, joked that the first recorded incident of non-compliance occurred when Eve defied God's prescription in the Garden of Eden and ate the apple.

Since then people have continued obstinately to defy the prescriptions of authorities, medical and otherwise. Indeed, non-compliance appears to be a very general feature of human behaviour. It is certainly observable in almost every area of therapeutic practice. We have already indicated the non-compliance rates in exercise programmes. Similar difficulties attend stress management and relaxation. For example, Hoelscher *et al.* (1986) reported that only 32 per cent of their fifty subjects practised relaxation daily as was advised. Other behavioural interventions also attract less than full compliance. Ley (1976), for example, reported an average drop-out rate from diet programmes of 49 per cent, and 51 per cent from various forms of counselling. Much of the research in this area has concentrated on medication and the extent to which patients fail to take prescribed medication properly, by which is meant taking too much, too little, taking it too irregularly, or ceasing taking their prescribed medicine altogether. The Food and Drug Administration of the United States (1979) cited the following percentages of non-compliance for a range of medications: antibiotics 48 per cent; psychoactive drugs 42 per cent; anti-hypertensive medication 43 per cent; anti-tuberculosis drugs 42 per cent; other medications 54 per cent. What is clear from these figures is that non-compliance is not only a feature of relatively minor complaints. Serious conditions, such as hypertension, are also frequently associated with low levels of compliance. The research regarding the pharmacological treatment of hypertension indicates that patients must take at least 80 per cent of prescribed medication in order to obtain maximum therapeutic benefit. In a recent study, Stanton (1987) found that as many as 46 per cent of patients took less than this criterion proportion of medication. Thus, for physicians, compliance continues to be an elusive goal.

What is Meant by Compliance

The term compliance is generally used to refer to the extent to which the patient's behaviour (in terms of taking medications, following diets, or executing other life style changes) coincides with medical or health instructions or prescriptions. However, Harvey (1988) has pointed out that there are considerable problems with the term 'compliance'. Implicit in the concept of compliance is the idea of physician authority and dominance and patient passivity and subservience. Thus, compliance implies a dependent layperson and a dominant professional, someone to issue instructions, and someone to carry them out. Doctor knows best and the patient ought to be doing as the doctor instructs. Failure to do so reflects some personal inadequacy on the part of the patient, i.e., the fault for non-compliance resides firmly with the patient.

Recently, in a well argued analysis, Trostle (1988) proposed that compliance, as usually conceived, is, in fact, an ideology, derived from presumptions about the proper relationships between physicians and other health professionals on one hand, and their clients or patients on the other. From this perspective, then, compliance can be regarded as a generally unhelpful concept, save in reinforcing the authority and power of physicians and other health care professionals. It is unhelpful, though, in the sense that when physicians label their patients as non-compliant they distance themselves from the patients' actions, judging them as wrong rather than analyzing and understanding what is going on. Thus, as indicated, non-compliance becomes an attribute of the patient, stemming from some flaw on his or her part, a characteristic of that patient's make-up and personality. This in turn has at least two consequences. Either it sponsors a search for those aspects of a patient's make-up that render them non-compliant, and, as we shall see, this has proved a rather fruitless activity, or, since people's personality is frequently regarded as immutable, it leads to the view that not much can be done. Harvey, while conceding that no truly satisfactory alternative exists, prefers the term adherence, following from Haynes' (1979) definition of adherence as the extent to which a person's behaviour coincides with medical or health advice. The word, advice, Harvey regards as important here, since advice is for considering and perhaps acting upon, whereas instructions are for following and prescriptions are for taking, both very much instances of passive obedience.

While matters of terminology and definition are far from trivial, what is crucial here is that conceptions of successful physician-patient interactions should characterize them as true interactions, and not one-way processes, the doctor telling the patient what to do, and that problems in physician-patient relationships do not inevitably stem from the patients' personality. After all, as Ley (1982) pointed out, health care professionals themselves do not always follow the best available recommendations about health, even when issuing advice to patients. Perhaps from this sort of perspective we shall get some answers to legitimate questions about the determinants of patients' health-related behaviours.

Such questions are not only legitimate but also important. As Trostle (1988) conceded,

> while compliance is an ideology, there are clinical, economic and academic reasons to study the use of medications. In the clinical realm, the irregular, diminished, or excessive consumption of medicine can reduce health or extend illness. Some medications must be taken long after symptoms disappear, others are dangerous if taken in excess, many are ineffective unless a certain critical minimum level of medication is taken.

Medication use that departs from recommendation may also result in increased health care expenditure. Although it is difficult to quantify precisely the costs, they are likely to be substantial. For example, Ausburn (1981) estimated the proportion of hospitalized patients whose hospitalization could be attributed to departing from earlier advice about medication. Twenty per cent of admissions, it was argued, were probably the result of such departures, with a further 5 per cent possibly the result.

Measurements of Adherence

Research in this area suffers not only from the problems of conceptual orientation addressed earlier. It also suffers from methodological difficulties. How precisely does one determine a patient's behaviour with regard to prescribed medication? A number of measures have been employed.

Undoubtedly the simplest and least intrusive is self-report, i.e., the patient is asked what they have done. In the main, this is not regarded as an accurate index. Few patients are willing to portray themselves in a negative light by admitting to departures from medical advice, i.e., there are strong social pressures to claim a close correspondence between what one was advised to do by health care professionals and what one did, irrespective of the actual reality of one's behaviour. In a similar fashion, physicians' estimates of patients' behaviour are often unreliable. Few physicians like to countenance the possibility that their patients have done other than what was advised. It would rather undermine their professional authority were they to admit otherwise.

Other methods involve the use of some form of pill count. The number of pills that remain in the patient's prescription by the presumed end of the course of the medication is one possibility here, as is a check with the pharmacy to determine when and if prescriptions have been refilled. In some cases special compartmentalized pill containers have been distributed to enable easy calculation of pills remaining. However, all these methods tell us only the amount of medication that has been used up and what, if anything, remains. They do not confirm that the patient has actually taken the medication. Patients can and do dispose of medication in ways other than their doctors intended.

A direct but intrusive method is to examine a patient's blood or urine for traces of a prescribed medication. This method is generally regarded as accurate. However, unless repeated measurements are taken, this method provides assessments of drug use only at a given point in time; for example, it cannot tell us whether a patient who registers the appropriate drug concentration in the urine has been taking the medication regularly or did so just prior to the assessment. In addition, as well as being a substantial imposition on patients, blood and urine analyses are costly and are not applicable to all drugs. As might be expected, less people are judged to have conformed to advice about medication by blood and urine analysis than by pill count methods, and less non-conformers are identified by self-report and physician report than by pill counts.

One final method which has been employed, particularly in areas such as hypertension, diabetes and obesity, is treatment overcome, i.e., if the patient has improved in line with clinical expectations, then adherence to the prescribed treatment or medication can be presumed. Conversely, lack of expected clinical gains would betoken imperfect adherence. The difficulties with this method are fairly self-evident. It presumes that treatment is 100 per cent effective and few, if any, medical or psychological interventions can boast anything close to perfect efficacy. In addition, a patient's progress is usually the function of a wide variety of factors, many of which have little to do with the elected therapy, even if it is generally effective with regard to the given complaint.

Varieties of Non-adherence

Before examining the evidence regarding what factors do and what factors do not relate to adherence, some general remarks are in order. One result of holding an overarching conception of compliance, and applying it in the manner in which it has been used, has been the tendency to lump all instances of therapeutic departure from advice and intention together. As Harvey (1988) pointed out, this is not only oversimplistic but retards progress in setting a proper agenda for research into patients' health behaviour.

It is obvious, for example, that different costs are involved in adhering to various prescriptions. For example, taking a short-term course of medication with few or no side effects differs from taking a long-term prescription with marked side effects which again differs from making permanent and substantial changes to life style. As indicated in a previous chapter, the personal and/or economic costs of major life style changes can be considerable and, in the case of people with few material resources, virtually prohibitive. Similarly, the seriousness and immediacy of the complaint is likely to have an effect. For example, Taylor *et al.* (1984) found that patients with cancer showed better than 90 per cent adherence rates to chemotherapy prescriptions. Only when these sorts of complexities are appreciated does it become possible to build and test sensible models of patients' behaviour.

In addition, it is important to distinguish varieties of non-adherence. Harvey (1988) provided a useful taxonomy here. For example, patients may decide that a particular recommended course of action is too difficult or involves too great an economic or a psychological cost, and so purposively fail to follow that course of action. This might be labelled deliberate or volitional non-adherence. Alternatively, the intricacies of a given prescription may be such that a patient forgets what precisely to do and when precisely to do it. Harvey referred to this as accidental non-adherence. Finally, the circumstances of the advised treatment may be such, for example the appearance of unsuspected but severe side effects, that intended adherence is jeopardized. Harvey called this circumstantial non-adherence. Again, this sort of analysis moves us on from the simplistic notion that patients are passive objects who either comply or do not comply with well-meaning, but ultimately authoritarian, medical instructions. It reveals non-adherence to be a much more complex matter, the product of a variety of circumstances and factors.

Factors that do not Relate to Adherence

The search for factors that affect adherence has been a highly energetic but not always particularly successful pursuit over the last ten years or so. This is unfortunate, since, as indicated previously, such a search is no empty academic inquiry. The identification of the factors involved is almost certainly an important step in the direction of improving the effectiveness of therapist-patient interaction and the quality of health care provision and delivery.

Haynes (1982) has identified some 250 variables which have been investigated in this context. These range from the personal, social and physical attributes of the patient, through the design of pill containers, to the influence of the weather. Given the prevailing conception of compliance it is perhaps by now hardly surprising to the reader that most of the studies have focused on patient attributes, the underlying presumption being that there is something odd about patients who fail to follow properly the instructions of their physician and that research in sufficient volume and of sufficient ingenuity will reveal the nature of the personal oddity or oddities. Perhaps this research effort would have been better served had it embarked from the presumption that all patients are potential non-adherers and that certain kinds of circumstances produce adherence. At any rate, few areas of inquiry have yielded so little on investment. Various reviews of the evidence indicate that no consistent predictors emerge from examination of the patients' personality or sociodemographic characteristics. In the main, gender, age, social class, education beyond a basic minimum, and a whole host of personality measures do not emerge as reliable correlates of adherence.

Clearly, research should now abandon its focus on patient attributes and discard the hypothesis that there are non-compliant sorts of people. The answers clearly lie elsewhere.

Factors that Relate to Adherence

Factors that have been identified as important in adherence have much more to do with the medical system itself, the patient's experience of it, his or her perception of the disease, and the extent and nature of the social support the patient receives from family and friends. Ley (1982) produced the following list of associated variables: duration and complexity of the treatment; patients' level of dissatisfaction with their doctor; absence of supportive follow-up; patients' perceptions of their vulnerability to the consequences of the illness; patients' perceptions of the seriousness of the illness; the perceived effectiveness of the treatment; the problems consequent on the treatment. Thus if the patient has to continue treatment for a long duration and treatment consists of having to take a number of drugs, adherence is likely to be relatively poor. Likewise if the patient receives little in the way of supportive supervision during the course of the treatment and is generally dissatisfied with the nature and quality of his or her relationship with the doctor, then adherence is again likely to be poor. On the other hand, higher levels of adherence are likely where the patient perceives the illness as serious and his or her personal vulnerability to be substantial. Finally, if the treatment causes problems, such as marked side effects, then adherence is likely to decline.

Ley could have added to this list the quality of the patient's social or family support. There is now a fair body of evidence to link such support with adherence. While some of this evidence is not without methodological problems, such as the difficulties involved in measuring adherence which have already been discussed, it does tend to point in the same general direction. Patients who have families and friends that offer positive support and show interest in the patients' condition and treatment tend to stick more closely to their prescriptions than those without such advantages. For example, Doherty *et al.* (1983) asked wives about their beliefs and behaviours relevant to their husbands' anti-hypertensive medication. Adherence was reliably better in men with supportive wives who believed in the benefits of the treatment. However, it was positive support that proved effective. Doherty *et al.* also found that where wives nagged their husbands about medication adherence was relatively poor.

The Health Belief Model and Adherence

Many of the factors that appear to be implicated in whether individuals conform or do not conform to medical advice sit well with the health belief model. I have already outlined the tenets of this model in the context of HIV/AIDS public health campaigns. Just to remind the reader, the model posits that whether health-promoting behaviour is adopted or not depends on the individual's perception of the severity of the complaint and his or her apparent vulnerability to it or its consequences. The individual then will weight the cost of any action undertaken against any benefits that may accrue. Finally, there must be some salient cue or prompt to action such as the appearance of symptoms or the availability of a screening programme or other public health initiative.

The health belief model was originally devised in the context of preventative health behaviour and public health campaigns. It has nonetheless been applied to the more specific issue of adherence to medical advice. As can be seen from the previous list of factors that appear to be implicated in adherence, it offers a reasonably sensible account. Both the patient's perception of the seriousness of the illness and his or her vulnerability to its consequences are involved in adherence in the manner that the model would predict. So too are the patient's perceptions of the effectiveness of the treatment and the problems or costs that may ensue. Thus, beliefs that treatment will benefit the condition substantially increase the likelihood of adherence, whereas any ambiguities about safety, side effects or distress associated with treatment reduce the likelihood that patients will do as advised.

However, it is clear that the health belief model will need revision in order to accommodate all the factors involved in adherence. For example, what broadly might be termed support seems to be an important factor. This emerges in three guises in the previous list. First of all, it may be viewed as a central determinant of patients' satisfaction or dissatisfaction with their physician. Broadly, it has been found that satisfactory consultations are those in which the physician appears supportive and caring. Physicians who adopt formal, business-like styles or are experienced as authoritarian and hostile tend to attract high levels of rated dissatisfaction. Second, physician support in terms of follow-up of the patient's progress would also appear to be implicated in adherence, and third, as I have illustrated, positive support from friends and family emerges as a factor, external to the consulting room or clinic, that seems to affect the patient's behaviour.

Understanding and Remembering Health Communications

There are two other, fairly self-evident, factors which affect whether or not patients follow the advice of their doctors. These are whether or not the patient has understood the advice that was offered and subsequently whether the patient has or has not remembered it. In fact, Ley (1982) has argued that variations in comprehension and memory account for much of the variation in adherence. Let us briefly consider these in turn.

Ley and Spelman (1967) listed three features of patient-doctor interaction that could contribute to the patient's not understanding the doctor's communications. First of all, the doctor's written or spoken advice may be just too difficult and complex. A number of studies have now applied readability formulae to standard medical and paramedical written material. Ley (1982) provided a summary of the outcome of these studies, which have examined among other things X-ray leaflets, prescription drug leaflets, health education material and optician leaflets. Overall, Ley's analysis indicated that only 20 per cent of the population would properly comprehend 75 per cent or more of this material. In contrast, 28 per cent of the population would understand 25 per cent or less of this material. In addition, Ley warns of problems that beset the application of such readability formulae. While a low score for readability nearly always indicates that something is wrong with written material as far as general comprehensibility is concerned, a high readability score can still characterize a leaflet that is hard to comprehend.

A second factor that can affect comprehension, according to Ley and Spelman, is the patient's lack of basic medical knowledge. Many people have difficulty even locating important bodily organs such as the heart, lungs, stomach or kidneys. Accordingly, comprehension would be well served by doctors not only producing material that is much more accessible, but also pausing to describe basic pertinent features of anatomy and physiology.

Finally, according to Ley and Spelman, patients often harbour ideas about disease and its origins that interfere with current medical theory and practice. Many people entertain folk theories of illness and its alleviation and in many cases this can be a barrier to following medical advice, when that advice runs counter to the folk theory. People are frequently reluctant to abandon their theories and remedies, often for good reason since they may have served them well in the past. Two examples will suffice to illustrate the powerful effect such theories can have on behaviour. Ankrah (1989) recently provided a harrowing account of the spread of HIV infection in Uganda. Briefly, AIDS was first diagnosed in Uganda in 1983 when residents of the fish landing ports of Lykunyu and Kasensero noticed that fishermen were afflicted with an illness that began with fever, followed by diarrhoea, skin rashes and wasting. Neither traditional nor modern medicine were able to prevent inevitable death. The local people believed that the fishermen were bewitched by Tanzanians. The fishermen smuggled goods across Lake Victoria in Tanzania, and it was believed that they had cheated the Tanzanians who had resorted to witchcraft in order to exact their revenge on the fishermen. Within a short time, though, it was noticed that the spouses and consorts of the fishermen began to display the same symptoms and die in the same circumstances. The particulars of the witchcraft theory were consequently amended, although the basic belief in witchcraft as the source of the misfortune remained intact. Local residents now believed that their whole communities had been bewitched. Acting on this belief an exodus started from Lukunyu and Kasensero, first to the neighbouring towns and then to the highway towns of Masaka and Lyantonde, and on to the capital, Kampala. Thus, as Ankrah concluded, it was the belief in and flight from witchcraft that contributed substantially to the initial spread of HIV infection in Uganda.

Moving from general health-related behaviour to the matter of adherence to medical advice, Gatchel *et al.* (1989) provide the example of a woman suffering from hypertension who failed to adhere properly to advice about medication, and took her medicine sporadically rather than regularly. The patient believed that whenever her blood pressure was elevated she suffered headaches. Accordingly, whenever she got a headache she would monitor her blood pressure, find it elevated, and take her medication. However, she did not take her blood pressure in the absence of headaches, and did not take her medication. Thus, as these authors pointed out, her selective monitoring of her blood pressure served to obscure the fact that her blood pressure was consistently elevated and that regular medication was required to manage it. Rather, her behaviour served her belief about the headache-blood pressure connection, which, in turn, dictated when she administered her medication.

Thus, it is important for physicians and others to appreciate that patients often possess elaborate, influential, and experientially-based lay theories of disease, symptomatology and treatment, and that effective consultation means that the physician or therapist must appreciate and be sensitive to such theories. Ignoring them or confronting them in a dismissive manner is unlikely to prove helpful. This reinforces the point I made earlier, that the process of medical consultation is one in which the patient should not be regarded as passive, but rather as cognitively and emotionally active, a person with a distinct social and psychological context and not merely a symptomatology.

Even if patients understand the advice offered them, they may subsequently forget much of it. Ley (1982) has summarized many of the studies that have been undertaken to assess patients' forgetting, and while results vary somewhat from study to study, most probably as a reflection of differences in methodology, there is still considerable consistency of outcome. Studies of mixed patient types attending general practices reveal that on average around 44 per cent of what they have been told by doctors is forgotten. The figure for a variety of patient types attending as medical outpatients at hospitals is again around 44 per cent. Surgical inpatients fare even worse; the analogous average figure is over 50 per cent. As Ley conceded, though, these figures were obtained from single consultations, i.e., one presentation of the information to be recalled. Where there is prolonged and repeated contact with the physicians, as in the case of pregnancy or in chronic conditions such as diabetes, recall rates are much higher, although still far from perfect.

While a number of psychological and demographic characteristics of patients have been investigated as potential determinants of forgetting, few consistent findings have emerged, although the level of patients' medical knowledge would seem to be implicated; high levels of knowledge are associated with better recall. In general, though, it would appear that forgetting has much more to do with the structure and complexity of the information than the nature of its recipient.

Concluding Remarks: Improving Adherence

The preceding discussion provides us with some clues as to how adherence might be improved. However, this is clearly a complex matter. Nevertheless, one of the messages that emerges is the need to abandon the rather authoritarian conception of compliance that has typically dominated much of the thinking and research in this area, with its implication that the origins of non-compliance are located in the patient's personality. The search for these personal oddities has proved fairly fruitless. Rather the roots of non-adherence would seem to be located in the nature of the interaction between patients, on one hand, and doctors and medical institutions on the other. Identified in the previous discussion as important are the patient's beliefs about illness and its causes, and how the physician understands and addresses these, the patient's perception of their own illness, its seriousness and likely consequences, his or her estimates of the potential success of the treatment advised and its likely personal and economic costs; also implicated is what the patient is told and how, and what support is available both from professionals and the patient's family and friends. It is attention to these sorts of factors that might yield dividends.

However, there is unlikely to be a universal solution. Low levels of adherence in different situations almost certainly arise from different combinations of these different influences. What this suggests is that a largely pragmatic approach is adopted. The way forward, I would argue, was illustrated some time ago by Finnerty *et al.* (1973a, 1973b) in a study concerned with the high drop-out rates from an inner-city hypertension programme. They started by attempting to discover what features of the medical context might be contributing to non-adherence, i.e., drop-out from the programme. They found that waiting time for an appointment, the lack of 24-hour availability of access, and variations in staff seen on different visits were major contributors to the initial 42 per cent clinic drop-out rate. When these were addressed, the drop-out rate fell to only 8 per cent. These will almost certainly not be the key factors in every circumstance. Far from it. But the study contains two lessons of real importance. First of all, it cautions us to begin from an analysis of the problem. Second, it suggests that the analysis might be most effectively focused on aspects of procedure and the patient's interaction with it, not on the personal characteristics of the patient.

Chapter 9

Pain and Psychological Approaches to its Management

Pain is a ubiquitous human experience. If one pauses momentarily to consider just one manifestation, headache, few of us seem not to have been affected at some time or other. In a survey conducted in 1970 of a random sample of people selected from the electoral register of Pontypridd in South Wales, Waters found that 65 per cent of the men and 79 per cent of the women surveyed reported that they had suffered from at least one headache in the previous year. The consequent economic costs are phenomenal. Rachman and Phillips (1978) cited an American study from as far back as 1968 which revealed that approximately sixteen million Americans were taking medication for headaches at an estimated annual cost of 400 billion dollars.

Pain and Injury

As Melzack and Wall (1988), in their invaluable book, *The Challenge of Pain*, pointed out, the link between pain and injury is so self-evident that it has nurtured the widely held belief that pain is the inevitable and exclusive result of physical damage, and that the intensity of pain we experience is directly proportional to the extent of the injury. Thus, it was believed that there was a direct and unerring psychophysical link between our personal pain experience on one hand and the physical properties of the damage we have sustained on the other; a small cut hurts a little and and a large wound hurts a lot. Pain, then, from this perspective, simply reflected the extent to which noxious stimulation impinges on the body's pain receptors. It was this kind of theory, known as specificity theory, that until recently informed much of medical and nursing practice. Thus, if a patient with substantial injury complained little of pain, he or she was regarded as 'being brave'. Conversely, patients with little tissue damage who complained of severe pain were regarded as 'making a fuss'.

However, even a superficial consideration of other modes of perception indicates that such a simple model of pain perception is unlikely to be adequate. In the case of visual perception, for example, it has long been clear that there is a vast amount of processing between the outside world and its stimulation of light receptors in the retina of our eyes, on the one hand, and our actual perceptions of objects and events on the other. Take, for example, a familiar coin and hold it 12 inches away from your eyes. Now hold it at full arm's length away. You will find that at the more distant position the coin appears only a little bit smaller than it does at the more proximal position. However, in terms of the stimulation that impinges on the receptors in the retina, the distant coin should appear about half the size of the coin when held at 12 inches. The reason for this is that we possess certain knowledges and beliefs about the properties of objects and the relationship between these properties. On the basis of such mental schemata, as they are sometimes called, adjustments are made to bring a certain consistency to our experience and perception of objects and events. In this particular case, mental schemata exist concerning the relationship between size and distance, and on the basis of these, compensations are made for distance by exaggerating the size of distant objects. This compensation is referred to as size constancy scaling and it operates to preserve the perceptual integrity of objects in spite of changes in their relationship to us.

Similar scaling operations serve to preserve other constancies. For example, snow viewed on a winter's evening reflects far less light onto the retinal receptors than does coal viewed on a summer's day. Yet we still perceive the coal as darker than the snow. As Keith Oakley (1972) eloquently pointed out, ambiguities such as these and the various visual illusions that we experience perform an important function by 'making strange' the all too familiar business of visual perception. This strangeness provides a way into the complex processes underlying perception and reminds us that perception is very much more than the literal translation of sensory stimulation into perceptual experience. Our knowledge, beliefs, desires, and needs all influence what we make of the patterns of stimulation our receptors receive from the world. There is no reason to believe that pain perception is any different in this regard, and substantial reasons for believing that psychological factors, such as beliefs and expectations, colour our perception of pain.

First of all, the relationship between pain and injury, i.e., between perception and pain receptor stimulation, is far from invariate. Some examples will serve to illustrate. The most common form of pain is tension headache, which ranges in severity from moderate to excruciating, yet there is no injury, no organic explanation for the pain. Trigeminal neuralgia is a rarer but even more severe variety of headache, in which even the mildest of stimuli applied to a trigger point on the face elicits an agonizing stab of pain as if the individual had been pierced by a knife. However, close scrutiny of the area of the pain reveals no tissue disorder or damage. Thus, intense pain can be experienced in the absence of apparent injury. Consideration of this issue might also include the curious case of phantom limb pain. Livingstone (1943), for example, reported the experience of a physician who had to have his arm amputated following a severe wound from a sharp scalpel. Subsequently, he often felt a piercing pain apparently coming from the site of the original injury. In intervals between these attacks of pain the physician reported a persistent painful burning in the amputated hand. Not only can pain be experienced in the absence of substantial injury, then, but it can also seem to arise from sites of the body that no longer exist.

In contrast, gross injury can occur in the absence of much in the way of pain. The most common example of this is what is called episodic analgesia. Beecher's (1956) report on his World War Two observations of the behaviour of soldiers who had been severely wounded provides a good example here. Beecher was surprised to find that most of the soldiers being brought to combat hospitals complained little of pain, in spite of being severely wounded. A formal comparison of the requests for pain-killing medication made by these soldiers with those made by civilians with comparable wounds as a result of surgery revealed striking differences in behaviour. Whereas more than 80 per cent of the civilian surgical patients requested medication, only 25 per cent of the combat-wounded soldiers did so. Beecher interpreted these results as clear evidence that psychological factors were mediating the pain experience. Specifically, he attributed the soldiers' relative failure to feel pain to their sense of relief at having escaped alive from combat in spite of their injury. Thus for the soldiers their injuries signified something positive. For the civilians, their surgical wounds would undoubtedly have different, less positive, meanings, such as loss of financial earnings.

Social and Psychological Influences on Pain

Beecher's research not only informs us that extensive injury can be sustained without severe pain, but also goes some way in identifying specific psychological factors that may be playing an important role in pain perception. There is a variety of other evidence that attests to the significance of social and cultural factors.

For example, cultural values are now recognized as having an important role to play in the way a person perceives and responds to pain. Melzack and Wall (1988) related the striking example of the hook-swinging ritual still practised in parts of India. A male person from the community is selected for the privilege of blessing the children and crops in a number of neigbouring villages. Steel hooks are inserted under the skin and muscle in the man's back. The hooks are then attached to strong ropes which are suspended from a beam that projects from a specially converted cart. The cart is driven from village to village and the blessings carried out. At the climax of each ceremony, the man swings free, back and forward, suspended only from the hooks embedded in his back. Nevertheless, the man gives no evidence of being in pain during these ceremonies; rather, according to Melzack and Wall, he appears to be in a state of exaltation.

Similarly, laboratory studies of pain tolerance suggest cultural and ethnic differences. Pain tolerance is defined for such purposes as the lowest intensity of some applied stimulus, such as an electric shock, at which an individual asks to have the stimulus withdrawn. Sternbach and Tursky (1965) found differences between groups of American women of different ethnic origins in terms of their capacity to tolerate electric shocks; women of Italian descent tolerated less shock than women of Jewish descent or what they called 'Yankee' women (Protestant women of British descent).

It is clear, then, that the psychological context of a painful stimulus can strongly affect pain experience and behaviour. Further examples of such effects come from studies of attention and distraction, and of stimulus control. If an individual's attention is directed towards a potentially painful event, this will tend to increase the severity of pain reported. Distraction, on the other hand, and the deliberate redirection of attention away from the potentially painful stimulus, serve to ameliorate the pain experience. Hall and Stride (1954), for example, reported that the mere appearance of the word 'pain' in a set of instructions caused subjects to describe as painful a level of electric shock that they did not consider painful when the word was missing from the instructions. This effect presumably resulted from the cue 'pain' focusing subjects' attention on the electric shock stimulus. Conversely, it is a common observation that pain is diminished when individuals are distracted or purposively distract themselves. Most parents rely heavily on distraction in attempting to comfort a child who has fallen and hurt himself or herself. Niven (1986) in a survey of young Scottish women found that distraction activities, usually involving keeping busy on other things, constituted the most frequently used coping strategy. However, laboratory research suggests that distraction is not always effective; it works mainly when pain is mild and short-lived.

There is now substantial evidence that responses to potentially painful stimulation are affected by whether or not there is the possibility of exercising control in the situation. Much of this evidence comes from laboratory studies comparing the relative impact of controllable and uncontrollable electric shocks. For example, in an early study Mowrer and Viek (1948) delivered electric shocks to two groups of laboratory rats while they were eating. One group could exercise control over the shocks by jumping into the air, while the other group could do nothing to escape the shocks. Although both groups received the same amount of shock during the experiment, the group with control ate more and showed less evidence of disturbance. In an analogous study on human subjects, Hokanson *et al.* (1971) had people perform an engaging mental task while receiving electric shocks. The shock schedules were arranged so that each subject on average received a shock every forty-five seconds. Subjects in one condition were allowed to take as many time-outs from the shock as they wished, and when they wished. Individuals in the other condition were 'yoked' to subjects in the first condition, such that they received the same number of time-outs at the same times, but had no choice in the matter. Measures of blood pressure indicated that the yoked subjects, i.e., those with no control, showed substantially higher blood pressures. That such physiological effects reflect differences in the perception of the painful stimulation is given weight by the findings of a study conducted by Staub *et al.* (1971). In the first part of the study, one group of subjects were given control over increases in the intensity of an electric shock on each trial. Yoked subjects in the other group were given no such facility but received shocks of the intensity that subjects in the other group had administered to themselves. Subjects who had control showed a reduced heart rate response to the shocks. In addition, subjects with control rated the shocks as less painful and showed a greater tolerance for shock than subjects without control. In the second part of the study, neither group were afforded control over the shocks. Compared to their own ratings in the first part of the study, subjects who had control removed rated the shocks as more painful and showed reduced tolerance in the absence of control.

The power of suggestion and the efficacy of placebos in moderating pain attest further to the role of psychological factors. Beecher (1959) reported that in instances of severe pain, such as post-surgical pain, patients often appear to gain relief from being given a placebo, some inert substance such as a sugar solution. Around 35 to 40 per cent of patients seem to benefit from such placebo treatment. As Melzack and Wall (1988) pointed out, this is a strikingly high proportion given that powerful analgesics such as morphine, even in large doses, relieve severe pain in only around 70 per cent of patients. Placebo effects are not just confined to instances of suggestion by medication; in fact, there is reason to believe that the more impressive and intrusive the thera-peutic procedure, the more likely it is to suggest effectiveness, irrespective of whether it actually exerts a direct effect on the patient's condition. For example, Beecher reported the outcomes of an operation that was at one time popularly applied to angina pectoris patients. Subsequent research into angina discredited this surgical procedure as being of no direct relevance to the condition. Nevertheless, a substantial number of patients gained relief from the pain of angina following the operation. One important characteristic in this regard was the surgeon's enthusiasm for the procedure; the rate of patients' relief was directly related to the surgeon's enthusiasm. Thus, the more a ther-apy impresses by its elaborateness and by the practitioner's belief and commit-ment, the more it is likely to promote effects solely through suggestion.

The Gate Control Theory of Pain

In an attempt to produce a theory of pain which admits such psychological influences and which regards pain perception as analogous to other modes of perception, in that a substantial amount of central processing and trans-formation separates the painful stimulus from our experience of pain, Melzack and Wall (1965) developed the gate control theory of pain.

The theory assumes that there are a number of structures and mechanisms in the nervous system that contribute to the perception of pain. Their interplay is crucial; pain is not the product of a simple transmission of stimulation from the skin or some internal organ to the brain. Key to this interactive process is the concept of the gate. Sensations from noxious stimulation impinging on pain receptors have to pass through the gate to the brain in order to emerge as pain perceptions. The status of the gate, though, is subject to a variety of influences, which can operate to shut the gate, thus inhibiting transmission, or cause it to be fully open, thus facilitating transmission. Accordingly, it is not merely the nature of the injury sustained and the accompanying sensations aris-ing at pain receptors that determine the perception of pain, but the particular disposition of the gate.

The position of the gate between fully opened or shut is determined by both peripheral and central influences. In the case of peripheral influences, competing sensations arising at the same time can act to reduce the pain from an injury or a noxious stimulus by operating to close the gate. It is a common tactic to rub one's arm when it has been bumped. Experience tells us that this serves to lessen the pain. Gate control theory postulates that this happens because the stimulation of rubbing inhibits the transmission of pain sensations by closing the gate. Central influences, arising in the brain, can also affect the gate. It is through this means that suggestion, expectation, belief, and other psychological factors modify pain perception. Most theories in psychobiology have a limited shelf life. Gate control theory is unlikely to be an exception. Nevertheless, it does account for many of the phenomena of pain experience in a way that the pain specificity approach does not.

One important recent discovery that may dramatically alter our understanding of the pain process is the discovery that our brains naturally produce opiate chemicals, i.e., substances akin to morphine. The first clue to their discovery was finding specific receptors in the brain that morphine molecules attached themselves to, and through this attachment exerted their powerful pain-killing effects. Why, though, should the brain possess receptors specialized for the reception of the morphine molecule? The answer, which emerged in the early 1980s, was that the body actually manufactured its own opiate substances, similar in structure to morphine, and that these receptors had evolved not in anticipation of the future discovery of morphine, but as part of an endogenous system, as receptors for internally produced opiates.

The term endorphins was coined to characterize these endogenous opiates, and their discovery raised a number of exciting issues. One immediately obvious possibility was that these endorphins mediated the placebo effect on pain. As indicated, inert substances and other procedures with no direct therapeutic effects can produce significant pain relief for up to 40 per cent of sufferers. There are some similarities between the operation of such placebos and narcotic analgesics such as morphine. For example, in both instances there is evidence of what is called tolerance; with repeated administration of either morphine or a placebo at a fixed dosage the analgesic effects decline. In addition, symptoms of withdrawal are apparent in both cases when their use is suddenly terminated.

More direct evidence of the involvement of endorphins in placebo effects emerges for studies using a drug called naloxone. Naloxone is an opiate antagonist, i.e., it operates to counter the effects of opiate drugs such as morphine. It also presumably blocks the effects of endorphins. In a study of postoperative dental pain, Levine *et al.* (1978) administered either placebo medication or naloxone to a group of patients three hours after a major tooth extraction. An hour later, patients received the other medication. The patients rated their pain following medication and a number of interesting findings emerged from analysis of these ratings. First of all, patients given naloxone at the outset reported greater pain than those who had received the placebo. Second, approximately 40 per cent of the patients reported pain relief with the placebo treatment. Finally, when naloxone was given as a second drug it produced ratings of increased pain in the patients who had gained relief from the placebo. These results are certainly consistent with the idea that endorphins are involved in placebo effects. In particular, the finding that placebo pain relief is curtailed by a drug that blocks the effects of endorphins, strongly implies that these naturally occurring endogenous opiates play an important role in the placebo phenomenon.

It should be noted that the presence and effects of endorphins do not undermine the gate-control theory. Rather, they suggest an additional chemical mechanism by which central, psychological factors might influence incoming sensations from pain receptors.

Assessment of Pain

The important role that psychological factors play in pain perception immediately raises the possibility that psychological techniques may be applied to its amelioration. Gate control theory clearly allows for such a possibility. In addition, the evidence relating to suggestion and placebo medication bears testimony to what are essentially psychological processes operating to produce pain relief in a not insignificant proportion of sufferers. Before considering how effective various psychological procedures are in pain management, it is perhaps worth saying something about the assessment of pain. After all, reliable and valid assessment is the cornerstone of any evaluation of therapeutic outcome.

However, assessing pain is no easy matter, since pain perception is a subjective phenomenon. We cannot inhabit another person's experiential world. We cannot feel their pain. The author for example, by virtue of gender, cannot experience menstrual cramps or feel labour pains! Accordingly, we have to rely on indirect methods of assessment: posing questions and making sense of the answers. However, apparently straightforward, open-ended questions such as 'How bad is the pain?' or 'What does it feel like?' are difficult to respond to, and it is difficult for the assessor to know what to make of the response. 'This is the worst pain I have ever experienced' may mean a lot to the respondent, but it is unlikely to make much sense to the assessor, since he or she has not had access to the respondent's previous history of pain. Fortunately other methods have been developed that attempt to impose more structure and system on inquiries about pain perception.

The two most frequently used are visual analogue scales and the McGill Pain Questionnaire (MPQ). The former consist of a series of horizontal lines of a given length, say 10 cm, with descriptors located at each end of a line as sort of verbal anchors, e.g., 'no pain' at one end and 'pain as severe as possible' at the other where pain intensity is the focus. The subject is asked to mark where on the line the pain they are currently experiencing lies. One advantage of a visual analogue scale approach is that it permits the quantification of any change in pain perception following, say, treatment by measuring the difference in length along the line between the subject's pre- and post-treatment marks. Another advantage is versatility. Different aspects of pain experience can be tapped by simply incorporating lines with different defining extremes. For example, in addition to pain intensity, a measure of the affective component of pain can be addressed by asking subjects to indicate how horrible their pain feels on a 10 cm line between the poles 'not horrible' and 'as horrible as possible'. There are reasons for believing that the intensity and affective dimensions of pain can vary independently. Morphine mainly appears to exert an influence on the affective dimension, such that the patient still feels the pain, but no longer regards it as so horrible (Bonnel *et al.*, 1988).

Also in widespread use is the MPQ. The MPQ consists of a series of descriptors, seventy-nine in all, arranged in twenty sections, where each section represents a different possible aspect of pain experience. For example, section 1 offers the following sensory adjectives: sickening, quivering, pulsing, throbbing, beating, pounding. Section 13 presents the following more affective descriptors: fearful, frightening, terrifying. As might be guessed from the two examples given, words are rank ordered within each section in terms of the severity of pain experience. The subject has to select which words best describe his or her pain, with the constraint that only one word can be chosen for any one section. Body maps are also provided to enable the individual to signify the site of the pain. (For a fuller description the reader is referred to Melzack and Wall, 1988.) The MPQ, then, allows the assessor to build up a detailed picture of the individual's pain experience, its site, its severity, and its affective and other characteristics. Melzack and Wall (1988) indicated that the MPQ discriminates well among what intuitively appear to be different sorts of pain experience. Briefly, the MPQ was administered to patients suffering from one of eight pain syndromes: neuralgia, phantom limb pain, pain associated with cancer, toothache, disease of the spinal discs, arthritis, labour pain, and menstrual pain. Each type of pain was found to have a distinct pattern of descriptors, which was used with remarkable consistency by different patients suffering from the same syndrome.

Other ways of measuring pain include the observation of pain behaviours such as grimacing, sighing, bracing, rubbing and the like. The problem with such external, more objective indices is that they may reflect things other than pain perception. However, they may contribute to the overall assessment, and provide useful measures when evaluating treatment outcome. This is particularly so in dealing with individuals suffering from chronic pain. For most of us, pain is a fleeting experience, the product of a minor injury that heals quickly. Even periods of longer-lasting and more intense pain, for example labour pains, although excruciating at the time, are relatively soon over. However, for some, pain is far from fleeting. Rather it is an enduring and consuming feature of their lives, directing their emotions and actions, colouring their views of their futures.

There is evidence that chronic pain brings with it a host of psychological problems that distinguish those afflicted from acute pain sufferers. Most importantly in the current context, as Harvey (1988) pointed out, the longer the period of pain, the longer the presence of pain behaviours, and the greater the opportunity that such behaviours, as public expressions of pain, will come to be directed by factors other than the pain experience. For example, behavioural expressions of pain are likely to elicit from others sympathy and attention and to merit exemption from arduous tasks. The longer this goes on the more these external influences will come to determine pain behaviour. A study conducted by Fordyce *et al.* (1979) nicely illustrates the point. A group of seventy-seven patients suffering from chronic pain were requested to perform a series of prescribed physical therapy exercises until pain, weakness or fatigue caused them to have to stop. There were a total of 442 occasions from these seventy-seven patients in which the number of repetitions of an exercise was recorded. Repetitions were then grouped according to the last digit, for example 11, 21, 31, etc. and 16, 26, 36, etc. These values were then further grouped into a 1 and 6 cluster, e.g., 11, 16, 26, etc., 2 and 7 cluster, e.g., 12, 22, 27, a 3 and 8 cluster, and so on. This yielded five final categories, the last of which consisted of repetitions that were multiples of 5, e.g., 5, 10, 15. Had the internal experience of pain been directing patients' behaviour then we would have expected each of these five categories to contain equivalent numbers of instances, i.e., patients would not have shown any numerical bias with regard to the last digit that characterized the repetition on which they ceased exercising. However, this was not the case. Rather, there was a massive over-representation of the last category. Approximately 50 per cent of these patients gave up exercising on a multiple of five repetitions. Thus patients seemed to be working towards a round figure, and not simply following the dictates of any internal pain perception. Their pain behaviour then, as represented here by exercise tolerance, was to a large extent a function of factors other than the experience of pain. This strongly suggests that therapeutic initiatives aimed at pain management might address pain behaviour as well as pain perception.

Psychological Approaches to Pain Management

Pain of a mild, short-lived and infrequently occurring character usually poses few problems. We usually either resort to a weak analgesic, such as aspirin, or simply wait it out, unaided by anything save stoicism. However, pain which is more intense and long-lasting, i.e., severe pain of either the protracted, chronic or persistently recurring variety, is a different matter.

Most of us have developed psychological strategies in the face of such pain. The two most popular habitual recourses are either to distraction or relaxation. However, the available evidence, as indicated previously, suggests that distraction is ineffective in such instances and works only with pain that is fleeting and mild. In addition, one of the shortcomings of relaxation as a strategy is that without assistance people are not, on the whole, particularly good at relaxing, especially when anxious and in pain. Accordingly, a variety of more formal procedures and technologies have been developed in order to assist people relax more deeply and reduce tension more effectively.

One of the most seemingly promising of these developments in recent years was biofeedback. I have already described biofeedback in the context of relaxation and blood pressure in Chapter 6, and reviewed its general clinical status elsewhere (Carroll, 1984). Here the focus will be on pain, and, more specifically, on the efficacy of biofeedback in combating recurrent and severe tension headaches. Muscle tension in the forehead and neck has been the usual target, with tension recorded and the information fed back to individuals in order to promote relaxation of the muscles at these sites. Early uncontrolled investigations were generally favourable, and suggested that with biofeedback individuals could learn to lower muscle tension and this was associated with reductions in the frequency (Budzynski *et al.*, 1970) and intensity (Wickrama-sekera, 1973) of headaches. However, subsequent, more controlled studies indicated a number of problems.

The requirement that efficacy be confirmed in the context of controlled studies is crucial. Without the surety provided by controlled clinical trials, the suspicion must always remain that any recorded improvement in a patient's condition arises from factors other than the influence of the particular therapy in question. Two noteworthy findings emerge from scrutiny of controlled studies in this area.

The first is that true muscle tension biofeedback appears to afford greater relief from headaches than false feedback. Thus, it would seem that more is at work here than the mere operation of expectancy. However, it remains unclear as to whether it is actual reductions in muscle tension that underlie the clinical gains. Consider the following study reported by Cram (1980). Thirty-two chronic headache sufferers were randomly assigned to one of four treatment groups. Group 1 patients were given muscle tension biofeedback; group 2 patients also received such feedback but with the instructions that they were not to use it to lower tension, but to stabilize tension at its relatively high initial levels; group 3 received false feedback and group 4 received no treatment whatsoever. Treatments lasted three weeks with two sessions per week. Only group 1 registered a significant reduction in muscle tension. However, with regard to headache activity, a different picture emerged. Patients in both groups 1 and 2 reported reliable reductions in headache activity. Thus muscle tension reduction through biofeedback might not be a necessary element. Rather, it might be the confirmation which feedback provides that the individual has exerted control over muscle tension, irrespective of the direction of control, that matters most. Certainly, feedback that one has successfully exercised control over some aspect of bodily functioning is an important and undoubtedly satisfying lesson. Perhaps, then, it is this indication of self-efficacy that, to an extent, underlies the reduction in headache symptoms. While issues such as this remain to be resolved, it would seem that, on balance, biofeedback does have a positive impact on tension headaches. However, is it any more successful in this regard than other, technologically less sophisticated, and cheaper means of promoting relaxation?

The second result that emerges from a consideration of controlled studies is that biofeedback is no more effective. Let us look at an example. Chesney and Shelton (1976) compared muscle tension biofeedback with a relaxation training programme which did not include a biofeedback facility. Headache sufferers were allocated to one of four groups: one group received biofeedback, a second undertook relaxation training, a third received biofeedback plus relaxation, and the fourth group were provided with no treatment. Only the relaxation training group and the relaxation plus biofeedback group benefited in terms of headache activity. Biofeedback on its own was far less effective. Other studies have also found that relaxation training does at least as well as biofeedback (see Carroll, 1984). Given equivalent efficacy, considerations of cost and ease of administration would argue for relaxation training, and against biofeedback, as the preferred treatment for severe and recurrent tension headache. Finally, there is evidence that relaxation training helps in a number of other areas, most noticeably in childbirth. Women who have undertaken relaxation training in preparation for childbirth generally report less labour pain than those who have not received such training (see Melzack and Wall, 1988). Moreover, relaxation training not only appears to reduce the affective dimension of pain, but also the sensory dimension, i.e., its intensity.

Since suggestion and the redirection of attention, as indicated earlier, have implications for pain perception and both are elements of hypnosis, we might expect that hypnosis would constitute an effective pain management strategy. While the hypnotic state defies precise definition, it would appear to comprise a trance-like state in which the subject's attention is focused intensely on the hypnotist, such that he or she is particularly receptive to suggestions made by the hypnotist. There is substantial laboratory evidence that susceptible individuals, once hypnotized, and given appropriate suggestions, can be administered quite intense stimulation, yet report experiencing no pain. In addition, there is a sizeable catalogue of clinical observations on the analgesic possibilities of hypnosis. Relief from pain by hypnosis has been reported in the areas of obstetrics, dentistry, surgery, and many more.

However, scepticism is likely to persist in the absence of a convincing account of how analgesia is achieved through hypnosis. We have some clues here, though, from the pioneering work of Hilgard (see Hilgard, 1977), which invokes the notion of a 'hidden observer'. Evidently many highly susceptible, highly hypnotizable subjects are able to respond to instructions, that on a given signal one of their hands will be liberated from the hypnotic state, and will write answers to specific questions posed, although the person will not be aware of what this liberated hand is doing. In experiments on hypnotic analgesia, for example, where the painful stimulus is ice-water, in which the other hand and arm is immersed, subjects are told that there is a part of the mind, 'the hidden observer', which can, by writing, communicate the true nature of their feelings. This part of the mind and the hand it controls are described as free from the hypnotist's suggestion about pain and analgesia.

In the non-hypnotic state, subjects report that immersion in the ice-water causes much pain. Once hypnotized and given a suggestion of analgesia that they will feel no pain, subjects actually report no pain from the immersion and behave as if no pain was being experienced. However, when the signal is given that the 'hidden observer' can now report, the relevant hand writes, in contrast, that the pain is severe, just as it was in the unhypnotized state, even though the subject is still insisting in his or her spoken description that no pain is being felt.

This implies that hypnotic analgesia may operate by influencing the evaluative and emotional significance of the painful stimulus. Somewhere, severe pain is registered, but the hypnotist's suggestion of analgesia causes the individual to dismiss this experience as undeserving of attention. This is perhaps akin to the way in which powerful chemical analgesics such as morphine work. As indicated previously they, too, appear mainly to influence the affective aspects of pain.

Finally, we have already noted similarities in the operation of morphine and placebo medication. Hypnosis and placebos would also seem to have much in common and, indeed, it has been argued (see, e.g., Barber, 1975) that hypnosis should not be regarded as a special state of mind. From this sort of perspective, hypnotic suggestion is just an instance of suggestion, and hypnotic induction an elaborate ritual for maximizing a subject's compliance to another's suggestion. Whatever turns out to be the case, both medical placebos and hypnosis appear to suffer from the same limitations as far as persistent and chronic pain is concerned, in that both may decline in effectiveness with repeated administrations. The reader will recall that this sort of tolerance effect is also a characteristic of morphine.

I have already indicated that behaviours which stem from suffering pain can, over time, become autonomous of that suffering, i.e., pain behaviours, driven initially by pain experience, come to be directed by external factors. One particular approach to the management of chronic pain takes as its target such pain behaviours.

Fordyce's (1982) work, with its aim of reducing pain behaviours, such as reliance on medication and physical inactivity, represents perhaps the clearest example of this type of approach. Chronic pain sufferers attend as outpatients for a period of between four and eight weeks. Medication use is monitored at entry to the programme and the patient allowed medication on request. The frequency of usage is noted. Subsequently, the medication schedule is changed by allowing medication only at fixed time intervals, the length of the interval depending on the average frequency of initial on-demand usage. Thus, the link between medication and pain is broken, and replaced by a time linkage. The intervals between medication delivery are then gradually increased, thus decreasing medication usage. The dosage level is also gradually reduced. To achieve this, the medication is offered as a cocktail, in, say, orange juice, and the medication component of the cocktail gradually lessened until it is only orange juice that is being administered. Patients' activity levels are increased in a largely analogous fashion. At the outset, patients are asked to exercise in a variety of ways until tolerance, i.e., until either pain or fatigue causes them to stop. On the basis of their average levels of activity at this stage, gradually increasing exercise targets are set and patients, by means of praise and other social rewards, such as feedback of performance, encouraged to achieve them. Throughout this programme rewards are orchestrated to reduce pain behaviour, and the patient's friends and family invited to participate, by making the attention, etc., that they give the patient, contingent on the absence of pain behaviours.

What evidence there is suggests that approaches such as this are successful in reducing medication, increasing physical capacity and generally reducing pain behaviours (see, e.g., Roberts and Reinhardt, 1980; Cincirpini and Floreen, 1982). For example, in a recent study Mayer *et al.* (1987) reported that of patients who had undergone a pain behaviour reduction programme 87 per cent were actively working compared to only 41 per cent of a no-treatment comparison group.

Concluding Remarks

Pain may be ubiquitous, but we have only recently come to understand something of its intricacies. Part of that understanding is that there is no simple, linear relationship between the sensory stimuli that impinge on pain receptors and our perceptual experience of pain. A host of psychological factors influence the transmission process and affect pain perception. In addition, pain perception is variably related to pain-related behaviours, and often these are driven by forces other than internal suffering.

From this understanding, we may be better able to develop appropriate methods of pain treatment and management. Given the role of psychological factors in both pain perception and pain behaviour it is almost certain that psychological intervention strategies will have a part to play. However, at present it is difficult to predict the precise nature of the part. In relaxation, hypnosis, suggestion, and the pragmatic approach to pain behaviour, illustrated by Fordyce's work, we have clues as to what might be effective with given individuals suffering from particular complaints. Herein lies a lesson. The tradition in medicine has been to seek a specific remedy for a specific condition. However, pain is not a homogeneous entity — a specific complaint. Not only are pain perception and pain behaviour complexly determined, but both are heterogeneous phenomena. Accordingly, we should beware of simple panaceas. It is more than likely that a combination of approaches is necessary in many instances. For example, it has been reported that the effects of analgesic medication are enhanced by the simultaneous administration of a placebo. Similarly, relaxation has been found to add to the effects of medication during childbirth. It is also almost certain that different approaches or combinations of approaches will work with different manifestations and types of pain. Fordyce's approach, for example, is most likely to be effective for patients who have suffered chronic pain for some time. In fact, his selection criterion specifically acknowledges this. Only patients who have been suffering pain for at least six months are admitted to treatment, and there must also be a demonstrable association between pain behaviours and external contingencies.

Chapter 10

Final Comments: Gender, Race, Social Class, and Health

The present text is very much meant as an introduction to the subject. No attempt has been made to offer encyclopaedic coverage, since this would have required several volumes of the present length. Instead, I have opted to discuss a discrete sample of topics within health psychology's broad remit, in the hope that such 'tasters' will encourage further inquiry. The areas I have chosen for inclusion very much reflect my own particular concerns and interests. While I hope that what I have included might be regarded as fairly central topics, I acknowledge that others would have made a different selection. I did aspire, though, to provide examples from what might be regarded as the two main strands of health psychology: the aetiological and the therapeutic. As the reader will recall from the opening chapter, health psychology has as its focus the contribution that the discipline of psychology has to make to our understanding of the onset and course of illness and disease on one hand and treatment, prevention, and health promotion on the other. I hope that, while I have probably not done proper justice to this diversity of purpose, I have at least given the reader a flavour of it.

Health psychology is not only relatively new, but it is also a rapidly evolving and changing discipline. While it is difficult to predict the precise directions this evolution will take, a number of issues seem increasingly to demand a prominent place on the agenda. Among these are issues of gender and race, and the potent influences on health stemming from broad social and material circumstances.

In the rest of this chapter, I will look in turn at each of these issues. Again, coverage will be necessarily brief. I suspect, though, that future health psychology texts will be much more occupied by matters of gender, race and social class than those which are currently available.

Gender Differences: Women's Health

Much of the research described in this text, especially in those chapters dealing with cardiovascular disease, has focused primarily on men. I should protest that this does not, for the most part, arise from any selective reporting on my part, but reflects a general preoccupation with males in many areas of health research. As Rodin and Ickovics (1990) pointed out, 'White men continue to be almost exclusively studied in major health care and pharmacological research. Even in animal-model research, male animals are almost always used.'

A number of justifications have been offered for this bias. Undoubtedly the most frequently voiced is the higher mortality rates for men in general, and from such causes as CHD in particular. In almost every decade of life men die at a greater rate than women. For CHD, the gender ratio for mortality is 2:1 in women's favour. However, men's disadvantage in this respect can hardly be regarded as a sound basis for excluding women from the study of diseases such as CHD. Indeed, there are several very persuasive reasons for their inclusion. First of all, in most western countries, CHD is the leading cause of death for women as well as for men. Second, by studying women and CHD, we may gain an insight into what is affording women their protective advantage, and this may yield dividends for both men and women. However, few studies have been devoted to this issue and many more are needed. Two major categories of explanation have been proposed for women's reduced CHD mortality: that women possess some sort of biological advantage; that women have a healthier lifestyle. Let me briefly consider these in turn.

It has been suggested that women's hormonal characteristics may afford them protection. Bush *et al.* (1987) compared the mortality rates from cardiovascular disease of women who were having oestrogen therapy following menopause with those of menopausal women who did not use oestrogen. They found that in every age category studied the oestrogen users had lower cardiovascular disease mortality rates, even after taking into account blood pressure and smoking differences. It has been proposed, therefore, that oestrogen may in general serve to reduce cholesterol levels. However, hypotheses that accord oestrogen a protective role of this sort have to contend with the results of studies on oral contraceptives (see Matthews, 1989b). Particularly when used by cigarette smokers, oral contraceptives, which are oestrogen-based, appear to increase the risk of CHD and stroke.

Another possibility is that women's hormones render them less responsive to psychological stress. Hastrup *et al.* (1980) and Hastrup and Light (1984) reported that women tested during the preovulatory phase of the menstrual cycle showed reduced cardiovascular reactions to psychological stress compared to women tested during the postovulatory phase and also compared to men tested on the same stressors. Stoney *et al.* (1988) also found that women tested during the preovulatory phase were less reactive than men. In a companion study Matthews and Stoney (1988) found that women were less reactive overall than men in terms of blood pressure.

However, others have not found any preovulatory reduction in reaction. For example, Carroll *et al.* (1984) tested women's heart rate reactions to laboratory stressors both preovulatory and postovulatory, with half the women being tested first during the preovulatory phase and half being tested first during the postovulatory phase. There was no overall difference in cardiac reaction between the two phases of the menstrual cycle. In fact, the most striking result of this study was the marked stability of individual variations in cardiac reactivity over time and menstrual cycle phase. To complicate matters even further, Polefrone and Manuck (1988) observed greater systolic blood pressure reactions to stress in women tested during the preovulatory phase of the menstrual cycle.

With regard to overall gender differences in cardiovascular reactions to stress, Stoney *et al.* (1987), following a review of the evidence, conclude that females display a tendency toward greater heart rate increase during stress compared to males; men, on the other hand, show higher systolic blood pressure reactions. This sort of complex effect also emerges from a more recent study by Stone *et al.* (1990); women showed relatively greater heart rate reactions to a video game stressor whereas men showed relatively higher systolic blood pressure reactions. However, again there are quite a number of exceptions to this general trend in results. For example, Van Doornen (1986) compared the reactions of men and women to a 'real-life' examination stress. Heart rate and systolic blood pressure were found to be much higher on the day of the examination compared to the levels recorded on a normal, routine day. However, there were no gender effects. The rise in activity during the day of the examination was of the same order for males and females.

While women's hormones may contribute to their protective advantage, there is, as yet, no clear evidence of what the mechanism might be, and it seems unlikely that oestrogen effects on cholesterol or differences in stress reactivity will provide a complete answer to the puzzle of gender differences in CHD mortality. Life style factors may also be involved.

In past years, men engaged in unhealthy behaviours to a far greater extent than women. As Rodin and Ickovics (1990) testified, there was at one time widespread social disapproval for women engaged in such activities as smoking and drinking excessively, whereas for men these were almost rites of passage. However, social expectations have changed, and these behaviours have become increasingly acceptable for women. Thus while men have, to an extent, started to moderate unhealthy activities of this sort, particularly cigarette smoking which is declining among men in many countries, women have shown almost the reverse trend, and in many western countries women's smoking rates continue to increase. If gender differences in mortality rates from such causes as CHD reflect differences in participation rates in unhealthy behaviours, we would expect, on the basis of more recent behavioural trends, to see a narrowing of the mortality gap. In fact, in some countries, such as the USA, the gender mortality gap is narrowing, especially for people 45 and older. Further, the male death rate from CHD has been slowly but steadily declining over recent years in many western countries, whereas no such decline is evident for women. Nevertheless, since gender mortality differences, including those for CHD, are still substantial, life style factors would again appear to provide only part of the answer.

Another possible explanation lies in the health-promoting effects of social support. There is now substantial evidence that low levels of social support are associated with poor physical and mental health. In the opening chapter of this text, I presented some illustrations of these effects. There is also evidence (see Baum and Grunberg, 1991; Shumaker and Hill, 1991) that women and men differ in terms of the character of their social support networks. Throughout life, girls and women are more likely to have confidantes than are boys and men. In adulthood, men frequently cite their spouses as their only confidantes, whereas women indicate spouses and friends with about the same frequency. Thus, in the main, women have more extensive and diverse social support available than men. Further, women generally report making more use of social support networks than men. It is probable that these variations in social support have consequences for mortality rates. However, in the absence of hard evidence, we can only guess at the extent of their influence.

Finally, there are two other important reasons why the study of women's health deserves a higher priority. First of all, there are a number of health concerns that are exclusive to women (breast and cervical cancer, hysterectomy, issues surrounding pregnancy and birth) or disproportionally affect women (rheumatoid arthritis, eating disorders). Health psychologists need to give much more attention to such conditions. Second, although women, as indicated, have lower mortality rates than men, they have higher levels of morbidity. Morbidity simply refers to ill-health, and almost every index of ill-health indicates that women suffer predominantly more than men: women consult physicians more often than men; they have higher levels of prescription and non-prescription drug use; they undergo more surgical procedures; in self-report studies, women report suffering from more illness than men. Thus although men have higher rates of the chronic diseases that constitute the leading causes of death, men are actually sick less often than women. A number of explanations have been offered for women's disadvantage in terms of morbidity: why they suffer more frequently than men from complaints that are serious but not necessarily life-threatening. It has been suggested, for example, that women are more sensitive than men to symptomatology and are more likely to report symptoms to a physician. It has also been suggested that women experience more psychological stress than men. There is certainly some evidence that women do report more stress. However, we are, as yet, without any satisfactory explanation for this apparent paradox. Answers when they come are likely to tell us things of general importance about the relationship between stress, behaviour, social support and disease.

Racial Differences in Health

In Chapter 9 I cited evidence that the experience of pain was affected by cultural factors, and that different ethnic groups within the USA varied in their tolerance of pain. Accordingly, it should come as no surprise to the reader that different ethnic and racial groups differ in terms of health generally and in their apparent vulnerability to particular diseases. In the preceding section I quoted Rodin and Ickovics's (1990) contention that health research, to date, has focused overmuch on men. Readers will recall that it was white men whom they identified as the overwhelmingly predominant objects of study. Just as it is necessary to redirect much of the research focus towards women, so blacks and other minority groups in western societies merit far more attention.

Let us consider one example where some redirection is occurring. Differences in blood pressure between blacks and whites in a number of communities are now well documented (see, e.g., N.B. Anderson, 1989). Epidemiological research has revealed a much higher incidence of hypertension in blacks in the USA, in some Caribbean countries, in urbanized areas of Africa, and, while far less research has been undertaken, in the UK. What is far from clear, though, is why blacks appear to be especially vulnerable in this respect.

A number of theories have been put forward. It has been suggested, for example, that blacks and whites show different patterns of cardiovascular reaction to psychological stress. The discussion of cardiovascular reactions to stress in Chapter 3 would lead to the expectation of higher heart rate and blood pressure reactions to stress among blacks, since I proffered a model of hypertension that linked its development to excessive cardiac reactions to psychological stress. However, the available data suggest otherwise. Either no consistent race effects have been found, or black hypertensive-risk subjects show smaller heart rate and systolic blood pressure increases to psychological stress than their white counterparts (for a review of the evidence, see N.B. Anderson *et al.*, 1989). For example Fredrikson (1986) examined various indices of cardiovascular reactivity to a stressful reaction-time task in hypertensive, borderline hypertensive (i.e., hypertensive-risk), and normotensive black and white Americans. Heart rate and systolic blood pressure reactions were greater in whites than blacks irrespective of blood pressure status. In addition, these reactions were affected by blood pressure status in the predicted direction, with normotensives showing the least reactivity. In contrast, though, vascular resistance measured in the skin and in the calf muscle increased in blacks but not white. Fredrikson interpreted his data as suggesting different blood pressure control mechanisms in blacks and whites, that whereas stress drives up blood pressure in whites largely through the cardiac mechanism described in Chapter 3, in blacks stress exerts its effects mainly on peripheral resistance. This notion that blood pressure elevation in blacks may be mediated by changes in resistance has been echoed elsewhere (e.g., Anderson *et al.*, 1988; Falkner and Kushner, 1989).

However, other explanations have been proposed. The most currently prominent among these emphasize coping styles among blacks that render them particularly vulnerable. For example, James and his associates (see, e.g., James *et al.*, 1983) have suggested that a psychological orientation which they label 'John Henryism' may be a key factor. Named after the legendary black folk hero, John Henry, it is epitomized by hard work and determined striving against overwhelming odds. It was hypothesized that those blacks who exhibited this type of determination with few positive resources (i.e., having low levels of formal education) would be particularly susceptible to hypertension. Some supporting evidence has been reported from a study of blacks in North Carolina. Those with relatively high scores on a scale measuring John Henryism and relatively low levels of formal education had the highest levels of blood pressure. One way of construing John Henryism and low resources is as an incongruity between the social position that one's hard work and striving merits and the position one actually occupies. For blacks in the West, racism is undoubtedly an important cause of such incongruity. Some support for this sort of interpretation emerges from a subsequent study by James *et al.* (1984). Black men with high John Henryism scores who felt that being black had hindered their chances of success had significantly higher blood pressure than their counterparts who felt that being black had actually helped them.

Another, and perhaps not wholly unrelated, sort of lifestyle incongruity, which appears to have implications for blood pressure in blacks, has been identified by William Dressler (e.g., Dressler, 1990). This incongruity Dressler defined as the extent to which life style (operationalized in terms of material possessions and exposure to cultural messages in the media) exceeds occupational status. In a sample of 186 black Americans, the greater the life style incongruity the greater the blood pressure. What Dressler's measure of life style incongruity most probably taps is the discrepancy between what people aspire to, in terms of life style (as evidenced by their material possessions), and the external construction of their social position (as determined by their occupational status and media portrayal of them). Thus even if one acquires the appropriate material accoutrements of a higher social rank, an incongruous occupational status can serve as a barrier. Viewed in this way, John Henryism and Dressler's life style incongruity are not so very far apart. Both would appear to embody a conflict between self-assessed merit on one hand (as a result of either industry and hard work, or material success) and externally represented social status on the other.

It could be argued that conflicts such as these are likely to elicit substantial feelings of anger and hostility, and that given constraints on expression, these feelings are more than likely to be suppressed. Harburg and his associates (e.g., Harburg *et al.*, 1979) have reported evidence of an association between suppressed hostility and high blood pressure in both blacks and whites. Although counter-evidence exists (Cochrane, 1973), there is nonetheless now a reasonable body of evidence linking habitual hostility and anger coping styles and hypertension (see, e.g., Diamond, 1982 for a review). Accordingly, the higher rates of hypertension among blacks may owe something to a prevalence of high levels of suppressed hostility. The barriers to social advancements that racism erects are likely to both elicit hostility and act as an obstacle to its expression.

Finally, there is strong evidence of a relationship between blood pressure and general socio-economic status, which holds for both blacks and whites; hypertension is much more prevalent in lower socio-economic groups (see, e.g., N.B. Anderson *et al.*, 1989). Concepts like John Henryism and Dressler's life style incongruity may be little more than broad descriptors of the frustrations faced by blacks at the lower ends of the social status ladder. Low socio-economic status undoubtedly brings with it a range of stressors (low income, unemployment, poor housing in areas of low social stability, high marital instability and so on). Given that blacks are proportionally more likely than whites to occupy lower socio-economic status positions in western societies, and have to face the added stresses that racism brings, it is perhaps hardly surprising that they suffer relatively high overall mortality rates and higher prevalences of chronic diseases such as hypertension.

Socio-economic Status and Health

The association between socio-economic status and hypertension is but one instance of a much broader phenomenon. In my concluding remarks to Chapter 6 I mentioned the link between social and material status and CHD. In general terms socio-economic status constitutes one of the most potent predictors of mortality.

In 1980, the so-called 'Black report' on social inequalities in health in the UK was published. It reported on an analysis of the relationship between mortality and social class, defined mainly in terms of occupational status, using data for the year 1971. The central result was that there were large differentials in health that favoured the higher social classes and that these were not being addressed in health and social policy. For example, for men aged 15–64 the standardized mortality rate in social class V (unskilled manual workers) was 1.8 times that in social class I (professional and managerial staff).

Since the publication of the Black report, additional information has become available in a number of areas. First of all, data have been collected on various indices of morbidity, which reveal that social class health differentials are not only manifest in the length of life, but also extend to the quality of life. Socio-economic status powerfully predicts the prevalence of a wide range of illnesses. Second, studies have now been undertaken in other countries with a similar social structure to the UK. These indicate the same broad trends. Third, results are now available from the examination of analogous data from 1981, ten years on from the Black report.

The Black report provided scant evidence on morbidity. However, we have already noted the social class gradient in blood pressure. Shaper *et al.* (1988) reported that British men in social class V on average registered systolic blood pressures more than 6 mm Hg higher than their counterparts in social class I. Similar class differentials have been reported for angina. Pocock *et al.* (1987) found almost twice the prevalence of angina among manual workers than among non-manual workers. A similar result emerged from a Welsh survey (Nutbeam and Catford, 1988). Subjects in social classes IV and V registered 50 per cent higher rates of angina than subjects from classes I and II. In areas of mental health, too, there is now substantial evidence that those lower down the socio-economic ladder suffer from more mental distress (see, e.g., Cochrane, 1983).

As indicated, comparative data are now available from several other countries. All point in the same general direction. For example, studies in Denmark, Finland, and Norway have found that the mortality rate for unskilled men was roughly twice that recorded for professional men with a university education. However, as Davey Smith *et al.* (1990) pointed out, the social class health gradients in the different countries vary somewhat, i.e., while social class variation in mortality rates is characteristic of all western countries, the magnitude of the differential differs between countries. There has been at least preliminary exploration of possible sources of such variation. What appears to be emerging from cross-national comparisons of this sort is that the steepness of social class mortality gradients reflects the magnitude of the disparities in income and wealth within a country, i.e., the extent of the differentials in mortality among social classes would seem to follow from the size of the inequalities in social and material provision among classes (Davey Smith *et al.*, 1990).

If this relationship is substantiated, it is clearly of enormous social and political significance. It indicates that, within the UK for example, as class disparities in income and material benefit increase so too will class health differentials. There is now evidence that social inequalities in health and well-being have been increasing in the UK since the publication of the Black report. Davey Smith *et al.* (1990) examined the data on social class and mortality for 1981. The social class-mortality gradient was even steeper than that found in 1971. For men aged 20–64 the mortality rate for men in social class V was now 2.4 times that recorded for men in social class I. Further, during the 1980s inequalities in income and material wealth have increased markedly in the UK. Accordingly, it is unlikely that the temporal trend identified by Davey Smith *et al.* will have abated. On the contrary, we would confidently predict that the 1991 data will reveal a further widening of the gap among social classes in morbidity and mortality.

As I indicated in Chapter 6, it has been argued that socio-economic and material effects can be reduced to matters of individual life style and, by implication, personal choice. Some behavioural risks, most noticeably those associated with unhealthy diets and smoking, are more prevalent in lower social class groups and undoubtedly this contributes to health and mortality differentials. However, there are two very good reasons why behavioural factors of this sort cannot provide a full account. First of all, as I indicated in Chapter 2, mortality rate variations with social status persist even when differences in behavioural risk are taken into account. Second, behavioural factors would appear to have a considerably stronger influence on the health of those in good material circumstances (Blaxter, 1990). As we have seen already, there is fairly convincing evidence that this is the case for type A behaviour: it would appear to be more of a CHD risk for those in non-manual occupations. Finally, it is a facile, but mistaken presumption that people's diets and smoking behaviour are purely matters of personal choice. Powerful social pressures and constraints are at work. People do not adopt and maintain their dietary and smoking habits in a vacuum. Poor material circumstances and limited access to transport manifestly restrict dietary choice. Cigarettes and other drugs of consolation are undoubtedly greater imperatives for those who have, by virtue of their poor social and material circumstances, greater need for solace.

Thus public health campaigns which urge those in poor circumstances to alter their life styles need to appreciate the complex determinants of unhealthy behaviours and the constraints facing even those who wish to follow the advice. All too often, though, such public urgings have been insensitive and patronizing, amounting to little more than exercises in victim-blaming and, at the same time, serving as convenient distractions from the realities of social and material inequality. However, even health promotion campaigns that are more sensitive, if focused entirely on behaviour, will only ever deal with part of the problem. The stresses and strains of impoverished social and material existences in the midst of affluence will persist. Were these to be tackled seriously, the benefits for health and well-being could be substantial.

Concluding Remarks

In this final chapter, I have attempted to predict what sorts of issues might preoccupy health psychologists in the near future. I have targeted gender, race, and social class as broad areas of study that I would certainly place high on the agenda. In addition, as indicated, HIV infection and AIDS will pose an increasing challenge. However, in making my forecast, I readily concede that there are numerous other, more circumscribed topics deserving of attention. Further, it is perhaps only fair to warn the reader that many health psychologists would disagree with or even take exception to the priorities I have identified. Nevertheless, I firmly believe that an increased concern with gender, race, and social class would yield enormous dividends for our understanding of the social, psychological, and psychobiological processes of illness and disease, and provide more informed guidance in matters of treatment, prevention and health promotion.

Bibliography

AGRAS, W.S., SOUTHAM, M.A. and TAYLOR, C.B. (1983) 'Long-term persistence of relaxation-induced blood pressure lowering during the working day', *Journal of Consulting and Clinical Psychology*, **51**, pp. 792–4.

ALFREDSSON, L., SPETZ, C.L. and THEORELL, T. (1985) 'Type of occupation and near-future hospitalization for myocardial infarction and some other diagnoses', *International Journal of Epidemiology*, **14**, pp. 378–88.

ANDERSON, B.L. (1989) 'Health psychology's contribution to addressing the cancer problem: Update on accomplishments', *Health Psychology*, **8**, pp. 683–703.

ANDERSON, B.L., ANDERSON, B. and DE PROSSE, C. (1989) 'Controlled prospective longitudinal study of women with cancer: II. Psychological outcomes', *Journal of Consulting and Clinical Psychology*, **57**, pp. 692–7.

ANDERSON, N.B. (1989) 'Racial differences in stress-induced cardiovascular reactivity and hypertension: Current status and substantive issues', *Psychological Bulletin*, **105**, pp. 89–105.

ANDERSON, N.B., LANE, J.D., TAQUCHI, F., WILLIAMS, R.B. and HOUSEWORTH, S.J. (1988) 'Racial differences in cardiovascular reactivity to mental arithmetic', *International Journal of Psychophysiology*, **6**, pp. 161–4.

ANDERSON, N.B., MYERS, H.F., PICKERING, T. and JACKSON, J.S. (1989) 'Hypertension in blacks: Psychosocial and biological perspectives', *Journal of Hypertension*, **7**, pp. 161–72.

ANKRAH, E.M. (1989) 'AIDS: Methodological problems in studying its prevention and spread', *Social Science and Medicine*, **29**, pp. 265–76.

ANTONI, M.H., AUGUST, S., LAPERRIERE, A., BAGGETT, H.L., KLIMAS, N., IRONSON, G., SCHNEIDERMAN, N. and FLETCHER, M.A. (1990) 'Psychological and neuroendocrine measures related to functional immune changes in anticipation of HIV-1 serostatus notification', *Psychosomatic Medicine*, **52**, pp. 496–510.

APPELS, A., MULDER, P. and VAN'T HOF, M. (1984) 'The predictive power of the A/B typology in Holland: Results of a 10-year follow-up study', paper presented at the conference, Biobehavioral Factors in Coronary Heart Disease, Winterscheid.

ARNETZ, B.B., WASSERMAN, J., PETRINI, B., BRENNER, S-O., LEVI, L., ENEROTH, P., SALOVAARA, H., HJELM, R., SALOVAARA, L., THEORELL, T. and PETTERSON, I-L. (1987) 'Immune function in unemployed women', *Psychosomatic Medicine*, **49**, pp. 3–11.

AUSBURN, L. (1981) 'Patient compliance with medical regimens', in SHEPPARD, J. (Ed.) *Behavioural Medicine*, Lidcombe, NSW, Cumberland College of Health Sciences.

BARBER, T.X. (1975) 'Responding to "hypnotic" suggestions: An introspective report', *American Journal of Clinical Hypnosis*, **30**, pp. 318–22.

BAREFOOT, J.C., DAHLSTROM, J.W. and WILLIAMS, R.B. (1983) 'Hostility, CHD incidence, and total mortality: A 25-year follow-up study of 255 physicians', *Psychosomatic Medicine*, **45**, pp. 59–63.

BAREFOOT, J.C., WILLIAMS, R.B., DAHLSTROM, W.G. and DODGE, K.A. (1987) 'Predicting mortality from scores of the Cook-Medley Scale: A follow-up of 118 lawyers', *Psychosomatic Medicine*, **49**, p. 210.

BAUM, A. and GRUNBERG, N.E. (1991) 'Gender, stress, and health', *Health Psychology*, **10**, pp. 80–5.

BEECHER, H.K. (1956) 'Relationship of significance of wound to the pain experienced', *Journal of the American Medical Association*, **161**, pp. 1609–13.

BEECHER, H.K. (1959) *Measurement of Subjective Responses*, Oxford, Oxford University Press.

BENNETT, P. and CARROLL, D. (1989) 'The assessment of type A behaviour: A critique', *Psychology and Health*, **3**, pp. 183–94.

BENNETT, P. and CARROLL, D. (1990) 'Type A behaviours and heart disease: Epidemiological and experimental foundation', *Behavioural Neurology*, **3**, pp. 261–77.

BENNETT, P., WALLACE, L., CARROLL, D. and SMITH, N. (1991) 'Treating type A behaviours and mild hypertension in middle-aged men', *Journal of Psychosomatic Research*, **35**, pp. 209–23.

BLANEY, N.T., MILLON, C., MORGAN, R., EISDORFER, C. and SZAPOCZNIK, J. (1990) 'Emotional distress, stress-related disruption and coping among healthy HIV-positive gay males', *Psychology and Health*, **4**, pp. 259–73.

BLAXTER, M. (1990) *Health and Lifestyle*, London, Tavistock.

BLIX, A.S., STROMME, S.B. and URSIN, H. (1974) 'Additional heart rate — an indicator of psychological activation', *Aerospace Medicine*, **45**, pp. 1219–22.

BLUMENTHAL, J.A., KONG, Y., SCHANBERG, S.M., THOMPSON, L.W. and WILLIAMS, R.B. (1978) 'Type A behavior and coronary atherosclerosis', *Circulation*, **58**, pp. 634–9.

BLUMENTHAL, J.A., BURG, M.M., BAREFOOT, J., WILLIAMS, R.B., HANEY, T. and ZIMET, C. (1987) 'Social support, Type A behavior, and coronary artery disease', *Psychosomatic Medicine*, **49**, pp. 331–9.

BLUMENTHAL, J.A., EMERY, C.F., WALSH, M.A., COX, D.R., KUHN, C.M., WILLIAMS, R.B. and WILLIAMS, R.S. (1988) 'Exercise training in healthy type A middle-aged men: Effects on behavioral and cardiovascular responses', *Psychosomatic Medicine*, **50**, pp. 418–33.

BONNEL, A.M., LUU, M. and BOUREAU, F. (1988) 'Multidimensional experimental pain study in normal man: Combining physiological and psychoindices', Meeting of the International Society for Psychophysics Conference, Stirling.

BORTNER, R.W. (1969) 'A short rating scale as a potential measure of pattern A behaviour', *Journal of Chronic Diseases*, **22**, pp. 87–91.

BROWN, G.W. and HARRIS, T. (1978) *Social Origins of Depression: A Study of Psychiatric Disorder in Women*, London, Tavistock.

BUDZYNSKI, T., STOYVA, J. and ADLER, C. (1970) 'Feedback induced muscle relaxation: Application to tension headache', *Journal of Behavior Therapy and Experimental Psychiatry*, **1**, pp. 205–11.

BUSH, L.T., CONNOR, B.E., COWAN, D.L., CRIQUI, H.M., WALLACE, D.R., SUCHINDRAN, M.C., TYROLER, A.H. and RIFKIND, M.B. (1987) 'Cardiovascular mortality and noncontraceptive use of estrogen in women: Results from the Lipids Research Clinics Program follow-up study', *Circulation*, **6**, pp. 1102–9.

BYRNE, D.G. (1981) 'Type A behaviour, life-events and myocardial infarction: Independent or related risk factors?', *British Journal of Medical Psychology*, **54**, pp. 371–7.

CANNON, W.B. (1935) 'Stresses and strains of homeostasis', *American Journal of Medical Sciences*, **189**, pp. 1 14.

CARROLL, D. (1984) *Biofeedback in Practice*, London, Longman.

CARROLL, D. and CROSS, G. (1990) 'The academics who double as electricians', *Independent*, 11 Oct., p. 23.

CARROLL, D., TURNER, J.R., LEE, H.J. and STEPHENSON, J. (1984) 'Temporal consistency of individual differences in cardiac response to a video game', *Biological Psychology*, **19**, pp. 81–93.

CARROLL, D., HEWITT, J.K., LAST, K., TURNER, J.R. and SIMS, J. (1985) 'A twin study of cardiac reactivity and its relationship to parental blood pressure', *Physiology and Behavior*, **34**, pp. 103–6.

CARROLL, D., CROSS, G. and HARRIS, M.G. (1990) 'Physiological activity during a prolonged mental stress test: Evidence for a shift in the control of pressor reactions', *Journal of Psychophysiology*, **4**, pp. 261–9.

CARROLL, D., HARRIS, M.G. and CROSS, G. (1991) 'Haemodynamic adjustments to mental stress in normotensives and subjects with mildly elevated blood pressure', *Psychophysiology*, **28**, pp. 439–47.

CASE, R.B., HELLER, S.S., CASE, N.B., MOSS, A.J. and the MULTICENTER POST-INFARCTION RESEARCH GROUP (1985) 'Type A behavior and survival after acute myocardial infarction', *New England Journal of Medicine*, **312**, pp. 737–41.

CHESNEY, M.A. and SHELTON, J.L. (1976) 'A comparison of muscle relaxation and electromyogram biofeedback treatments for muscle contraction headache', *Journal of Behavior Therapy and Experimental Psychiatry*, **7**, pp. 221–5.

CHESNEY, M.A., HECKER, M.H.L. and BLACK, G.W. (1988) 'Coronary-prone components of type A behavior in the WCGS: A new methodology', in HOUSTON, B.K. and SNYDER, C.R. (Eds) *Type A Behavior Pattern, Research, Theory, and Intervention*, New York, Wiley.

CHIN, J. (1990) 'Current and future dimensions of the HIV/AIDS pandemic in women children', *Lancet*, **336**, pp. 221–4.

CINCIRPINI, P.M. and FLOREEN, A. (1982) 'An evaluation of a behavioral program for chronic pain', *Journal of Behavioral Medicine*, **5**, pp. 375–89.

COCHRANE, R. (1973) 'Hostility and neuroticism among unselected essential hypertensives', *Journal of Psychosomatic Research*, **17**, pp. 215–18.

COCHRANE, R. (1983) *The Social Creation of Mental Illness*, London, Longman.

COHEN, J.B. and REED, D. (1985) 'The type A behavior pattern and coronary heart disease among Japanese men in Hawaii', *Journal of Behavioral Medicine*, **8**, pp. 343–52.

COOPER, M.I. (1982) 'Effect of relaxation on blood pressure and serum cholesterol', *Activitus Nervosa Superior*, **Suppl. 3**, pp. 428–36.

CRAM, J.R. (1980) 'EMG biofeedback and the treatment of tension headaches: A systematic analysis of treatment components', *Behavior Therapy*, **11**, pp. 699–710.

CULL, A. (1990) 'Invited review: Psychological aspects of cancer and chemotherapy', *Journal of Psychosomatic Research*, **34**, pp. 129–40.

DANTZER, R. and KELLEY, K.W. (1989) 'Stress and immunity: An integrated review of relationships between the brain and the immune system', *Life Sciences*, **44**, pp. 1995–2008.

DATTORE, P., SHONTZ, F. and COYNE, L. (1980) 'Premorbid personality differentiation of cancer and non-cancer groups', *Journal of Consulting and Clinical Psychology*, **48**, pp. 388–94.

DAVEY SMITH, G., BARTLEY, M. and BLANE, D. (1990) 'The Black report on socioeconomic inequalities in health 10 years on', *British Medical Journal*, **301**, pp. 373–7.

DEAN, C. and SURTEES, P.G. (1989) 'Do psychological factors predict survival in breast cancer', *Journal of Psychosomatic Research*, **33**, pp. 561–9.

DEBACKER, G., KORNITZER, M., KITTEL, F. and DRAMAIX, M. (1983) 'Behavior, stress and psychological traits as risk factors', *Preventive Medicine*, **12**, pp. 32–6.

DE GEUS, E.J.C., VAN DOORNEN, L.J.P., DE VISSER, D.C. and ORLEBEKE, J.F. (1990) 'Existing and training induced differences in aerobic fitness: Their relationship to physiological response patterns during different types of stress', *Psychophysiology*, **27**, pp. 457–78.

DEMBROSKI, T.M., MACDOUGALL, J.M., WILLIAMS, R.B., HANEY, T.L. and BLUMENTHAL, J.A. (1985) 'Components of type A, hostility, and anger-in: Relationships to angiographic findings', *Psychosomatic Medicine*, **47**, pp. 219–33.

DEPARTMENT OF HEALTH AND SOCIAL SECURITY (1980) *Inequalities in Health: Report of a Research Working Group* (Black Report), London, DHSS.

DIAMOND, E.L. (1982) 'The role of anger and hostility in essential hypertension and coronary heart disease', *Psychological Bulletin*, **92**, pp. 410–33.

DIMSDALE, J.E., HACKETT, T.P., CATANZANO, D. and WHITE, P.J. (1979) 'The relationship between diverse measures for type A personality and coronary angiographic findings', *Journal of Psychosomatic Research*, **23**, pp. 289–93.

DIMSDALE, J.E., BLOCK, P.C., GILBERT, J., HACKETT, T.P. and HUTTER, A.M. (1981) 'Predicting cardiac morbidity based on risk factors and coronary angiographic findings', *American Journal of Cardiology*, **47**, pp. 73–6.

DOHERTY, W.J., SCHROTT, H.G., METCALF, L. and IASIELLO-VALLAS, L. (1983) 'Effect of spouse support and health beliefs on medication adherence', *Journal of Family Practice*, **17**, pp. 837–41.

DRESSLER, W.W. (1990) 'Lifestyle, stress, and blood pressure in a southern black community', *Psychosomatic Medicine*, **52**, pp. 182–98.

DUBBERT, P.M., MARTIN, J.E., ZIMERING, R.T., BURKETT, P.A., LAKE, M. and CUSHMAN, W.C. (1984) 'Behavioral control of mild hypertension with aerobic exercise: Two case studies', *Behavior Therapy*, **15**, pp. 373–80.

FALKNER, B. and KUSHNER, H. (1989) 'Race differences in stress-induced reactivity in young adults', *Health Psychology*, **8**, pp. 613–27.

FALKNER, B., KUSHNER, H., ONESTI, G. and ANGELAKOS, E.T. (1984) 'Cardiovascular characteristics in adolescents who develop essential hypertension', *Hypertension*, **6**, pp. 301–6.

FINNERTY, F., MATTIE, E.C. and FINNERTY, F.A. (1973a) 'Hypertension in the inner city: I. Analysis of clinic drop-outs', *Circulation*, **47**, pp. 73–5.

FINNERTY, F., SHAW, L. and HIMMELSBACK, C. (1973b) 'Hypertension in the inner city: II. Detection and follow-up', *Circulation*, **47**, pp. 76–8.

FOLKINS, C.H. and SIME, W.E. (1981) 'Physical fitness training and mental health', *American Psychologist*, **36**, pp. 378–389.

FONTANA, A.F., KERNS, R.D., ROSENBERG, R.L. and COLONESE, K.L. (1989) 'Support, stress, and recovery from coronary heart disease: A longitudinal causal model', *Health Psychology*, **8**, pp. 175–93.

FOOD AND DRUG ADMINISTRATION (1979) 'Prescription drug products: Patient labelling requirements', *Federal Register*, **44**, pp. 40016–40041.

FORDYCE, W.E. (1982) 'A behavioural perspective on chronic pain', *British Journal of Clinical Psychology*, **21**, pp. 313–20.

FORDYCE, W.E., CALDWELL, L. and HONGADAROM, T. (1979) 'Effects of performance feedback on exercise tolerance in chronic pain', unpublished manuscript, University of Washington, Washington, Seattle.

FOX, B.H. (1978) 'Premorbid psychological factors as related to cancer incidence', *Journal of Behavioral Medicine*, **1**, pp. 45–133.

FRANCIS, K.T. (1979) 'Psychologic correlates of serum indicators of stress in man: A longitudinal study', *Psychosomatic Medicine*, **41**, pp. 617–28.

FRANK, K.A., HELLER, S.S., KORNFELD, D.S., SPORN, A.A. and WEISS, M.B. (1978) 'Type A behavior and coronary angiographic findings', *Journal of the American Medical Association*, **240**, pp. 761–3.

FREDRIKSON, M. (1986) 'Racial differences in cardiovascular reactivity to stress in essential hypertension', *Journal of Hypertension*, **4**, pp. 325–31.

FREDRIKSON, M. and MATTHEWS, K.A. (1990) 'Cardiovascular reactivity to mental stress in arterial hypertension: A meta-analytic review', *Annals of Behavioral Medicine*, **12**, pp. 30–9.

FRENCH-BELGIAN COLLABORATIVE GROUP (1982) 'Ischaemic heart disease and psychological patterns: Prevalence and incidence studies in Belgium and France', *Advances in Cardiology*, **29**, pp. 25–31.

FRIEDMAN, M., THORESEN, C.E., GILL, J.J., ULMER, D., POWELL, L.H., PRICE, V.A., BROWN, B., THOMPSON, L., RABIN, D., BREALL, W.S., BOURG, E., LEVY, R. and DIXON, T. (1986) 'Alteration of Type A behavior and its effects on cardiac recurrences in postmyocardial infarction patients: Summary of the Recurrent Coronary Prevention Project', *American Heart Journal*, **112**, pp. 653–65.

GATCHEL, R.J., BAUM, A. and KRANTZ, D.S. (1989) *An Introduction to Health Psychology*, New York, Random House.

GLASS, D.C. and SINGER, J.E. (1972) *Urban Stress*, New York, Academic Press.

GRAY-TOFT, P. and ANDERSON, J.G. (1981) 'The nursing stress-scale: Development of an instrument', *Journal of Behavioral Assessment*, **3**, pp. 11–23.

GREER, S. and BRADY, M. (1988) 'Natural killer cells: One possible link between cancer and the mind', *Stress Medicine*, **4**, pp. 105–11.

GREER, S. and MORRIS, T. (1975) 'Psychological attributes of women who develop breast cancer: A controlled study', *Journal of Psychosomatic Research*, **19**, pp. 147–53.

GUYTON, A.C., COLEMAN, T.G., BOWER, J.D. and GRANGER, H.J. (1970) 'Circulatory control in hypertension', *Circulation Research*, **27**, **Suppl. II**, pp. 135–48.

HALL, K.R.L. and STRIDE, E. (1954) 'The varying response to pain in psychiatric disorders: A study in abnormal psychology', *British Journal of Medical Psychology*, **27**, pp. 48–60.

HARBURG, E., BLAKELOCK, E.H. and ROPER, P.J. (1979) 'Resentful and reflective coping with arbitrary authority and blood pressure: Detroit', *Psychosomatic Medicine*, **41**, pp. 189–202.

HARVEY, P. (1988) *Health Psychology*, London, Longman.

HASTRUP, J.L. and LIGHT, K.C. (1984) 'Sex differences in cardiovascular stress responses: Modulation as a function of menstrual cycle phases', *Journal of Psychosomatic Research*, **28**, pp. 475–83.

HASTRUP, J.L., LIGHT, K.C. and OBRIST, P.A. (1980) 'Relationship of cardiovascular stress response to parental history of hypertension and to sex differences', *Psychophysiology*, **17**, pp. 317–18.

HAYNES, R.B. (1979) 'Introduction', in HAYNES, R.B., SACKETT, D.L. and TAYLOR, D.W. (Eds) *Compliance in Health Care*, Baltimore, Johns Hopkins University Press.

HAYNES, R.B. (1982) 'Improving patient compliance', in STUART, R.B. (Ed.) *Adherence, Compliance, and Generalization in Behavioral Medicine*, New York, Brunner Mazel.

HAYNES, S.G., LEVINE, S., SCOTCH, N., FEINLEIB, M. and KANNEL, W.B. (1978) 'The relationship of psychosocial factors to coronary heart disease in the Framingham study. I: Methods and risk factors', *American Journal of Epidemiology*, **107**, pp. 362–83.

HENRY, J.P., ELY, D.L., WATSON, F.M.C. and STEPHENS, P.M. (1975) 'Ethological methods as applied to the measurement of emotion', in LEVI, L. (Ed.) *Emotions: Their Parameters and Measurement*, New York, Raven.

HILGARD, E.R. (1977) *Divided Consciousness: Multiple Controls in Human Thought and Action*, New York, Wiley.

HOELSCHER, T.J., LICHSTEIN, K.L. and ROSENTHAL, T.L. (1986) 'Home relaxation practice in hypertension treatment: Objective assessment and compliance induction', *Journal of Consulting and Clinical Psychology*, **54**, pp. 217–21.

HOKANSON, J.E., DEGOOD, D.E., FORREST, M.S. and BRITTAIN, T.M. (1971) 'Availability of avoidance behaviors in modulating vascular-stress responses', *Journal of Personality and Social Psychology*, **19**, pp. 60–8.

HOLMES, D.S. (1983) 'An alternative perspective concerning the differential psychophysiological responsivity of persons with the type A and type B behavior patterns', *Journal of Research in Personality*, **17**, pp. 40–7.

HOUSE, J.S., MCMICHAEL, A.J., WELLS, J.A., KAPLAN, B.H. and LANDERMAN, L.R. (1979) 'Occupational stress and health among factory workers', *Journal of Health and Social Behaviour*, **20**, pp. 139–60.

HOUSTON, B.K. (1983) 'Psychophysiological responsivity and the type A behavior pattern', *Journal of Research in Personality*, **17**, pp. 22–39.

IRONSON, G., LAPERRIERE, A., ANTONI, M.H., O'HEARN, P., SCHNEIDERMAN, N., KLIMAS, N., CAROLIS, P. and FLETCHER, M.A. (1990) 'Changes in immune and psychological measures as a function of anticipation and reaction to news of HIV-1 antibody status', *Psychosomatic Medicine*, **52**, pp. 247–70.

IRVINE, M.J., JOHNSTON, D.W., JENNER, D.A. and MARIE, G.V. (1986) 'Relaxation and stress management in the treatment of essential hypertension', *Journal of Psychosomatic Research*, **30**, pp. 437–50.

IRWIN, M. (1988) 'Depression and immune function', *Stress Medicine*, **4**, pp. 95–103.

JACOBS, M.A., SPILKEN, A. and NORMAN, M. (1969) 'Relationship of life change, maladaptive aggression and upper respiratory infection in male college students', *Psychosomatic Medicine*, **31**, pp. 33–42.

JAHODA, M. and RUSH, H. (1980) 'Work, employment and unemployment: An overview of ideas and research results in the social science literature', Science Policy Unit, Occasional Paper Series No. 12.

JAMES, S.A., HARTNETT, S.A. and KALSBECK, W.D. (1983) 'John Henryism and blood pressure differences among black men', *Journal of Behavioral Medicine*, **6**, pp. 259–78.

JAMES, S.A., LACROIX, A.Z., KLEINBAUM, D.G. and STROGATZ, D.S. (1984) 'John Henryism and blood pressure differences among black men: II. The role of occupational stressors', *Journal of Behavioral Medicine*, **7**, pp. 259–75.

JANSEN, M.A. and MUENZ, L.R. (1984) 'A retrospective study of personality variables associated with fibrocystic disease and breast cancer', *Journal of Psychosomatic Research*, **28**, pp. 35–42.

JENKINS, C.D., ROSENMAN, R.H. and FRIEDMAN, M. (1967) 'Development of an objective psychological test for the determination of the coronary-prone behavior pattern in employed men', *Journal of Chronic Diseases*, **20**, pp. 371–9.

JENKINS, C.D., ROSENMAN, R.H. and ZYZANSKI, S.J. (1976) 'Risk of new myocardial infarction in middle-aged men with manifest coronary heart disease', *Circulation*, **53**, pp. 342–7.

JENKINS, C.D., ZYZANSKI, S.J. and ROSENMAN, R.H. (1979) *Jenkins Activity Survey Manual*, New York, Psychological Corporation.

JOHNSON, E.H., GANT, L., JACKSON, L., GILBERT, D. and WILLIS, C. (1991)

'Multiple sex partners, knowledge about AIDS, and attitudes about using condoms among black males', paper presented at the annual meeting of the Society of Behavioral Medicine, Washington, DC.

JOHNSTON, D.W., COOK, D.G. and SHAPER, A.G. (1987) 'Type A behaviour and ischaemic heart disease in middle aged British men', *British Medical Journal*, **295**, pp. 86–9.

JOHNSTON, D.W., ANASTASIADES, P. and WOOD, C. (1990) 'The relationship between cardiovascular responses in the laboratory and in the field', *Psychophysiology*, **27**, pp. 34–44.

KAMARCK, T.W., MANUCK, S.B. and JENNINGS, J.R. (1990) 'Social support reduces cardiovascular reactivity to psychological challenge: A laboratory model', *Psychosomatic Medicine*, **52**, pp. 42–58.

KANNEL, W.B. (1977) 'Importance of hypertension as a major risk factor in cardiovascular disease', in GENET, J., KOIW, E. and KUCHEL, O. (Eds) *Hypertension, Pathology and Treatment*, New York, McGraw-Hill.

KIECOLT-GLASER, J.K., GLASER, R., STRAIN, E., STOUT, J., TARR, K., HOLLIDAY, J. and SPEICHER, C. (1986) 'Modulation of cellular immunity in medical students', *Journal of Behavioral Medicine*, **9**, pp. 5–21.

KIECOLT-GLASER, J.K., FISHER, L.D., OGROCKI, P., STOUT, J.C., SPEICHER, C. E. and GLASER, R. (1987) 'Marital quality, marital disruption, and immune function', *Psychosomatic Medicine*, **49**, pp. 13–34.

KISSEN, D. (1963) 'Personality characteristics in males conducive to lung cancer', *British Journal of Medical Psychology*, **36**, pp. 27–36.

KRANTZ, D.S. and MANUCK, S.B. (1984) 'Acute psychophysiologic reactivity and risk of cardiovascular disease: A review and methodologic critique', *Psychological Bulletin*, **96**, pp. 435–64.

KRANTZ, D.S., MATTHEWS, K.A., SANMARCO, M.E. and SELVESTER, R.H. (1979) 'Psychological correlates of progression of atherosclerosis in men', *Psychosomatic Medicine*, **41**, pp. 467–75.

KRANTZ, D.S., DAVIA, J.E., DEMBROSKI, T.M., MacDOUGALL, J.M., SHAFFER, R.T. and SCHAEFFER, M.A. (1981) 'Extent of coronary atherosclerosis: Type A behaviour, and cardiovascular response to social interaction', *Psychophysiology*, **18**, pp. 654–64.

LAZARUS, R.S. (1966) *Psychological Stress and the Coping Process*, New York, McGraw-Hill.

LAZARUS, R.S. and COHEN, J.B. (1977) 'Environmental stress', in ATTMAN, I. and WOHLWILL, J.F. (Eds) *Human Behavior and the Environment: Current Theory and Research*, New York, Plenum.

LAZARUS, R.S., OPTON, E.M., JR., NOMIKOS, M.S. and RANKIN, N.O. (1965) 'The principle of short-circuiting of threat: Further evidence', *Journal of Personality*, **33**, pp. 622–35.

LEVINE, J.D., GORDON, N.W. and FIELDS, H.L. (1978) 'The mechanisms of placebo analgesia', *Lancet*, **ii**, pp. 654–7.

LEY, P. (1976) 'Towards better doctor-patient communication: Contributions from social and experimental psychology', in BENNETT, A.E. (Ed.) *Communications between Doctors and Patients*, London, Nuffield Provincial Hospitals Trust.

LEY, P. (1982) 'Satisfaction, compliance, and communication', *British Journal of Clinical Psychology*, **21**, pp. 241–54.

LEY, P. and SPELMAN, M.S. (1967) *Communicating with the Patient*, London, Staples Press.

LIGHT, K.C., KOEPKE, J.P., OBRIST, P.A. and WILLIS, P.W. (1983) 'Psychological stress induces sodium and fluid retention in men at high risk for hypertension', *Science*, **220**, pp. 429–31.

LIGHT, K.C., OBRIST, P.A., JAMES, S.A. and STROGATZ, D.S. (1987) 'Cardiovascular responses to stress: II. Relationships to aerobic exercise patterns', 'Psychophysiology', **24**, pp. 79–86.

LIVINGSTONE, W.K. (1943) *Pain Mechanisms*, New York, Macmillan.

LOVALLO, W.R. and PISHKIN, V. (1980) 'A psychophysiological comparison of Type A and B men exposed to failure and uncontrollable noise', *Psychophysiology*, **17**, pp. 29–36.

MacDOUGALL, J.M., DEMBROSKI, T.M., DIMSDALE, J.L. and HACKETT, T.P. (1985) 'Components of type A, hostility, and anger-in: Further relationships to angiographic findings', *Health Psychology*, **4**, pp. 137–52.

McKIRNAN, D.J. and PETERSON, P.L. (1989) 'AIDS-risk behavior among homosexual males: The role of attitudes and substance abuse', *Psychology and Health*, **3**, pp. 161–71.

MANN, A.W. and BRENNAN, P.J. (1987) 'Type A behaviour score and the incidence of cardiovascular disease: A failure to replicate the claimed associations', *Journal of Psychosomatic Research*, **31**, pp. 685–92.

MANUCK, S.B., KAPLAN, J.R. and CLARKSON, T.B. (1983) 'Behaviorally induced heart rate, reactivity and atherosclerosis in cynomolgus monkeys', *Psychosomatic Medicine*, **45**, pp. 95–108.

MANUCK, S.B., KAPLAN, J.R., ADAMS, M.R. and CLARKSON, T.B. (1989) 'Behaviorally elicited heart rate reactivity and atherosclerosis in female cynomolgus monkeys (*Macaca fascicularis*)', *Psychosomatic Medicine*, **51**, pp. 306–18.

MARMOT, M.G., SHIPLEY, M.J. and ROSE, G. (1984) 'Inequalities in health-specific explanations of a general pattern?' *Lancet*, **i**, pp. 1003–6.

MATARAZZO, J.D. (1980) 'Behavioral health and behavioral medicine: Frontiers of a new health psychology', *American Psychologist*, **35**, pp. 807–17.

MATTHEWS, K.A. (1982) 'Psychological perspectives on the type A behavior pattern', *Psychological Bulletin*, **91**, pp. 293–323.

MATTHEWS, K.A. (1989a) 'Are sociodemographic variables markers for psychological determinants of health?', *Health Psychology*, **8**, pp. 641–8.

MATTHEWS, K.A. (1989b) 'Interactive effects of behavior and reproductive hormones on sex differences in risk for coronary heart disease', *Health Psychology*, **8**, pp. 373–87.

MATTHEWS, K.A. and STONEY, C.M. (1988) 'Influences of sex and age on cardiovascular responses during stress', *Psychophysiology*, **50**, pp. 46–56.

MATTHEWS, K.A., GLASS, D.C., ROSENMAN, R.H. and BORTNER, R.W. (1977) 'Competitive drive, pattern A., and coronary heart disease: A further analysis of some data from the Western Collaborative Group Study', *Journal of Chronic Disease*, **30**, pp. 923–60.

MAYER, T.G., GATCHEL, R.J., MAYER, H., KISHINO, N., KELLY, J. and MOONEY, V. (1987) 'A prospective two-year study of functional restoration in industrial low back injury utilizing objective assessment', *Journal of the American Medical Association*, **258**, pp. 1763–7.

MEDICAL RESEARCH COUNCIL WORKING PARTY (1985) 'MRC trial of treatment of mild hypertension: Principal results', *British Medical Journal*, **291**, pp. 97–104.

MELZACK, R. and WALL, P. (1965) 'Pain mechanisms: A new theory', *Science*, **150**, pp. 971–9.

MELZACK, R. and WALL, P. (1988) *The Challenge of Pain*, Harmondsworth, Penguin.

MESULAM, M.M. and PERRY, J. (1972) 'The diagnosis of love-sickness: Experimental psychophysiology without the polygraph', *Psychophysiology*, **9**, pp. 546–51.

MIRSKY, I.A. (1958) 'Physiologic, psychologic, and social determinants in the etiology of duodenal ulcer', *American Journal of Digestive Diseases*, **3**, pp. 285–314.

MORRIS, J.N., EVERITT, M.G., POLLARD, R., CHAVE, S.P.W. and SEMMENCE, A. M. (1980) 'Vigorous exercise in leisure-time: Protection against coronary heart disease', *Lancet*, **ii**, pp. 1207–10.

MORRIS, T., GREER, S., PETTINGALE, R.W. and WATSON, M. (1981) 'Patterns of expression of anger and their psychological correlates in women with breast cancer', *Journal of Psychosomatic Research*, **25**, pp. 111–17.

MOSES, J., STEPTOE, A., MATHEWS, A. and EDWARDS, S. (1989) 'The effects of exercise training on mental well-being in the normal population: A controlled trial', *Journal of Psychosomatic Research*, **35**, pp. 47–61.

MOWRER, O.H. and VIEK, P. (1948) 'An experimental analogue of fear from a sense of helplessness', *Journal of Abnormal and Social Psychology*, **43**, pp. 193–200.

MULDOON, M.F., MANUCK, S.B. and MATTHEWS, K.A. (1990) 'Lowering cholesterol concentrations and mortality: A quantitative review of primary prevention trials', *British Medical Journal*, **301**, pp. 309–14.

MULLEADY, G. (1987) 'A review of drug abuse and HIV infection', *Psychology and Health*, **1**, pp. 149–63.

MULTICENTER POSTINFARCTION RESEARCH GROUP (1983) 'Risk stratification and survival after myocardial infarction', *New England Journal of Medicine*, **309**, pp. 331–6.

MYRTEK, M. and GREENLEE, M.W. (1984) 'Psychophysiology of type A behavior pattern: A critical analysis', *Journal of Psychosomatic Research*, **28**, pp. 455–66.

NIVEN, C. (1986) 'Factors affecting labour pain', unpublished PhD thesis, University of Stirling.

NORRIS, R., CARROLL, D. and COCHRANE, R. (1990) 'The effects of aerobic and anaerobic training on fitness, blood pressure, and psychological stress and well-being', *Journal of Psychosomatic Research*, **34**, pp. 367–75.

NORRIS, R., CARROLL, D. and COCHRANE, R. (1992) 'The effects of physical activity and exercise training on psychological stress and well-being in an adolescent population', *Journal of Psychosomatic Research*, **36**, pp. 55–65.

NUTBEAM, D. and CATFORD, J. (1988) *Pulse of Wales: Social Survey Supplement*, Cardiff, Heartbeat Wales.

OATLEY, K. (1972) *Brain Mechanisms and Mind*, London, Thames and Hudson.

OBRIST, P.A. (1976) 'The cardiovascular behavioral interaction — as it appears today', *Psychophysiology*, **13**, pp. 95–107.

OBRIST, P.A. (1981) *Cardiovascular Psychophysiology: A Perspective*, New York, Plenum Press.

O'LEARY, A., JEMMOTT, L.S., BOOCHER-LATTIMORE, D. and GOODHART, F. (1991) 'Condom use by New Jersey college students: A social cognitive analysis', paper presented at the annual meeting of the Society of Behavioral Medicine, Washington, DC.

ORNISH, D., BROWN, S.E., SCHERWITZ, L.W., BILLINGS, J.H., ARMSTRONG, W. T., PORTS, T.A., MCLANAHAN, S.M., KIRKEEIDE, R.L., BRAND, R.J. and GOULD, K.L. (1990) 'Can lifestyle change reverse coronary heart disease?', *Lancet*, **336**, pp. 129–33.

ORTH-GOMER, K. and UNDEN, A-L. (1990) 'Type A behavior, social support, and coronary risk: Interaction and significance for mortality in cardiac patients', *Psychosomatic Medicine*, **52**, pp. 59–72.

PAFFENBARGER, R.S., HALE, W., BRAND, R. and HYDE, R.J. (1977) 'Work-energy level, personal characteristics and fatal heart attack: A birth-cohort effect', *American Journal of Epidemiology*, **105**, pp. 200–13.

PATEL, C.H. (1975) 'Twelve-month follow-up of yoga and biofeedback in the management of hypertension', *Lancet*, **i**, pp. 62–4.

PATEL, C.H. and NORTH, W.R.S. (1975) 'Randomized controlled trial of yoga and biofeedback in management of hypertension', *Lancet*, **ii**, pp. 93–5.

PATEL, C.H., MARMOT, M.G. and TERRY, D.J. (1981) 'Controlled trial of biofeedback-aided behavioural methods in reducing mild hypertension', *British Medical Journal*, **282**, pp. 2005–8.

PATEL, C., MARMOT, M.G., TERRY, D.J., CARRUTHERS, M., HUNT, B. and PATEL, M. (1985) 'Trial of relaxation in reducing coronary risk: Four-year follow-up', *British Medical Journal*, **290**, pp. 1103–6.

PERSKY, V.W., KEMPTHORNE-RAWSON, J. and SHEKELLE, R.B. (1987) 'Personality and risk of cancer: 20-year follow-up of the Western Electric study', *Psychosomatic Medicine*, **49**, pp. 435–49.

PETTINGALE, K.W., GREER, S. and TEE, D.E.H. (1977) 'Serum IgA and emotional expression in breast cancer patients', *Journal of Psychosomatic Research*, **21**, pp. 395–9.

PETTINGALE, K.W., PHILALITHISA, A., TEE, D.E.H. and GREER, S. (1981) 'The biological correlates of psychological responses to breast cancer', *Journal of Psychosomatic Research*, **25**, pp. 453–8.

PETTINGALE, K.W., MORRIS, T., GREER, S. and HAYBITTLE, J.L. (1985) 'Mental attitudes to cancer: An additional prognostic factor', *Lancet*, **i**, p. 750.

PHILLIPS, K. (1988) 'Strategies against AIDS', *The Psychologist*, Feb., pp. 46–7.

PHILLIPS, K. and WHITE, D. (1991) 'AIDS: Psychological, social and political reactions to a modern epidemic', in COCHRANE, R. and CARROLL, D. (Eds) *Psychology and Social Issues*, London, Falmer Press.

POCOCK, S.J., SHAPER, A.G., COOK, D.G., PHILLIPS, A.N. and WALKER, M. (1987) 'Social class differences in ischaemic heart disease in British men', *Lancet*, **ii**, pp. 197–201.

POLEFRONE, J.M. and MANUCK, S.B. (1988) 'Effects of menstrual phase and parental history of hypertension on cardiovascular response to cognitive challenge', *Psychosomatic Medicine*, **50**, pp. 23–36.

POOLING PROJECT RESEARCH GROUP (1978) 'Relationship of blood pressure, serum cholesterol, smoking habit, relative weight and ECG abnormalities to incidence of major coronary events: Final report of the pooling project', *Journal of Chronic Diseases*, **31**, pp. 201–306.

RACHMAN, S.J. and PHILLIPS, C. (1978) *Psychology and Medicine*, Harmondsworth, Penguin.

RAGLAND, D.R. and BRAND, R.J. (1988) 'Type A behavior and mortality from coronary heart disease', *New England Journal of Medicine*, **318**, pp. 65–9.

RAHE, R.H. (1975) 'Life changes and near-future illness reports', in LEVI, L. (Ed.) *Emotions: Their Parameters and Measurements*, New York, Raven.

RAHE, R.H., MAHAN, J.L. and ARTHUR, R.J. (1970) 'Prediction of near-future health changes from subjects' preceding life changes', *Journal of Psychosomatic Research*, **14**, pp. 401–6.

REVIEW PANEL ON CORONARY-PRONE BEHAVIOR AND CORONARY HEART DISEASE (1981) 'Coronary-prone behavior and coronary heart disease: A critical review', *Circulation*, **63**, pp. 1199–1215.

RIGBY, K., BROWN, M., ANAGNOSTOU, P., ROSS, M.W. and ROSSER, B.R.S. (1989) 'Shock tactics to counter AIDS: The Australian Experience', *Psychology and Health*, **3**, pp. 145–59.

RILEY, V., FITZMAURICE, M.A. and SPACKMAN, D.H. (1981) 'Animal models in biobehavioral research: Effects of anxiety stress on immunocompetence and neoplasia', in WEISS, S.M., HERD, J.A. and FOX, B.H. (Eds) *Perspectives in Behavioral Medicine*, New York, Academic Press.

ROBERTS, A. and REINHARDT, L. (1980) 'The behavioral management of chronic pain: Long term follow-up with comparison groups', *Pain*, **8**, pp. 151–62.

RODIN, J. and ICKOVICS, J.R. (1990) 'Women's health: Review and research agenda as we approach the 21st century', *American Psychologist*, **45**, pp. 1018–34.

ROSENMAN, R.H. (1978) 'The interview method of assessment of the coronary-prone behaviour pattern', in DEMBROSKI, T.M., WEISS, S.M., SHIELDS, J.L., HAYNES, S.G. and FEINLEIB, M. (Eds) *Coronary-prone Behavior*, New York, Springer-Verlag.

ROSENMAN, R.H., BRAND, R.J., JENKINS, C.D., FRIEDMAN, M., STRAUS, R. and WURM, M. (1975) 'Coronary heart disease in the Western Collaborative Group Study: Final follow-up experience of 8½ years', *Journal of the American Medical Association*, **22**, pp. 872–7.

ROSKIES, E., KEARNEY, H., SPEVACK, M., SURKIS, A., COHEN, C. and GILMAN, S. (1979) 'Generalizability and duration of treatment effects in an intervention program for coronary prone (Type A) managers', *Journal of Behavioral Medicine*, **2**, pp. 195–207.

SAKAKIBARA, T. (1966) 'Effects of brightness or darkness on carcinogenesis', *Nagoya Shiritsz Daigaku igakkai Sasshi*, **19**, pp. 525–47.

SCHERG, H. and BLOHMKE, M. (1988) 'Association between selected life events and cancer', *Behavioral Medicine*, **14**, pp. 119–24.

SCHERWITZ, L., MCKELVIAN, R., LAMAN, C., PATTERSON, J., DUTTON, L., YUSIM, S., LESTER, J., KRAFT, W., ROCHELLE, D. and LEACHMAN, R. (1983) 'Type A behavior, self-involvement, and coronary atherosclerosis', *Psychosomatic Medicine*, **45**, pp. 47–57.

SCHERWITZ, L., GRAHAM, L.E., GRANDITS, G. and BILLINGS, J. (1987) 'Speech characteristics and behavior-type assessment in the Multiple Risk Factor Intervention Trial (MRFIT) Structured Interviews', *Journal of the American Medical Association*, **233**, pp. 872–7.

SCHLEIFER, S.J., KELLER, S., MCKEGNEY, F. and STEIN, M. (1980) 'Bereavement and lymphocyte function', paper presented at the Annual Meeting of the American Psychiatric Association, Montreal.

SEEMAN, T.E. and SYME, S.L. (1987) 'Social networks and coronary artery disease: A comparison of the structure and function of social relations as predictors of disease', *Psychosomatic Medicine*, **49**, pp. 341–54.

SELWYN, P. (1986) in MCCONNELL, H. 'Forcing drug abusers to make decisions', *The Journal*, 1 Jan., p. 3.

SHAPER, A.G., ASHBY, D. and POCOCK, S. (1988) 'Blood pressure and hypertension in middle-aged British men', *Journal of Hypertension*, **6**, pp. 367–74.

SHAPIRO, A.P., NICOTERO, J., SAPIRA, J. and SCHEIB, E.T. (1968) 'Analysis of the variability of blood pressure, pulse rate, and catecholamine resprosivity in identical and fraternal twins', *Psychosomatic Medicine*, **30**, pp. 506–20.

SHEKELLE, R.B., RAYNOR, W.J., OSTFELD, A.M., GARRON, D.C., BIELIANSKAS, L.A., LIU, S.C., MALIZA, C. and PAUL, O. (1981) 'Psychological depression and 17-year risk of death from cancer', *Psychosomatic Medicine*, **43**, pp. 117–25.

SHEKELLE, R.B., BILLINGS, J.H., BORHANI, W.O., GERACE, T.A., HULLEY, S.B., JACOBS, D.R., LASSER, N.L., MITTLEMARK, M.B., NEATON, J.D. and STAMLER, J. (1985a) 'The MRFIT behavior pattern study: II. Type A behavior and incidence of coronary heart disease', *American Journal of Epidemiology*, **122**, pp. 559–70.

SHEKELLE, R.B., GALE, M. and NORUSIS, M. for the ASPIRIN MYOCARDIAL INFARCTION STUDY RESEARCH GROUP (1985b) 'Type A score (Jenkins Activity Survey) and risk of recurrent coronary heart disease in the Aspirin Myocardial Infarction Study', *American Journal of Cardiology*, **56**, pp. 221–5.

SHERR, L. (1987) 'An evaluation of the UK government health education campaign on AIDS', *Psychology and Health*, **1**, pp. 61–72.

SHERWOOD, A., ALLEN, M.T., OBRIST, P.A. and LANGER, A.W. (1986) 'Evaluation of beta-adrenergic influences on cardiovascular and metabolic adjustments to physical and psychological stress', *Psychophysiology*, **23**, pp. 89–104.

SHERWOOD, A., LIGHT, K.C. and BLUMENTHAL, J.A. (1989) 'Effects of aerobic exercise training on hemodynamic responses during psychosocial stress in normotensive and borderline hypertensive type A men: A preliminary report', *Psychosomatic Medicine*, **51**, pp. 123–36.

SHUMAKER, S.A. and HILL, D.R. (1991) 'Gender differences in social support and physical health', *Health Psychology*, **10**, pp. 102–11.

SIMS, J. and CARROLL, D. (1990) 'Cardiovascular and metabolic activity at rest and during psychological and physical challenge in normotensives and subjects with mildly elevated blood pressure', *Psychophysiology*, **27**, pp. 149–56.

SINYOR, D., GOLDEN, M., STEINERT, Y. and SERAGANIAN, P. (1986) 'Experimental manipulation of aerobic fitness and response to psychosocial stress: Heart rate and self-report measures', *Psychosomatic Medicine*, **48**, pp. 324–37.

STANTON, A.L. (1987) 'Determinants of adherence to medical regimens by hypertensive patients', *Journal of Behavioral Medicine*, **10**, pp. 377–94.

STAUB, E., TURSKY, B. and SCHWARTZ, G.E. (1971) 'Self-control and predictability: The effects on reactions to aversive stimulation', *Journal of Personality and Social Psychology*, **18**, pp. 157–62.

STEPTOE, A. (1984) 'Psychophysiological processes in disease', in STEPTOE, A. and MATHEWS, A. (Eds) *Health Care and Human Behaviour*, London, Academic Press.

STEPTOE, A., EDWARDS, S., MOSES, J. and MATHEWS, A. (1989) 'The effects of exercise training on mood and perceived coping ability in anxious adults from the general population', *Journal of Psychosomatic Research*, **33**, pp. 537–47.

STEPTOE, A., MOSES, J., MATHEWS, A. and EDWARDS, S. (1990) 'Aerobic fitness, physical activity, and psychophysiological reactions to mental tasks', *Psychophysiology*, **27**, pp. 264–74.

STERNBACH, R.A. and TURSKY, B. (1965) 'Ethnic differences among housewives in psychophysical and skin potential responses to electric shock', *Psychophysiology*, **1**, pp. 241–6.

STONE, S.V., DEMBROSKI, T.M., COSTA, P.T., JR. and MACDOUGALL, J.M. (1990) 'Gender differences in cardiovascular reactivity', *Journal of Behavioral Medicine*, **13**, pp. 137–57.

STONEY, C.M., DAVIS, M.C. and MATTHEWS, K.A. (1987) 'Sex differences in physiological responses to stress and in coronary heart disease: A causal link?', *Psychophysiology*, **24**, pp. 127–31.

STONEY, C.M., MATTHEWS, K.A., MCDONALD, R.H. and JOHNSON, C.A. (1988) 'Sex differences in lipid, lipoprotein, cardiovascular, and neuroendocrine responses to acute stress', *Psychophysiology*, **25**, pp. 645–56.

STROMME, S.B., WIKEBY, P.C., BLIX, A.S. and URSIN, H. (1978) 'Additional heart rate', in URSIN, H., BAADE, E. and LEVINE, S. (Eds) *Psychobiology of Stress*, London, Academic Press.

SUINN, R. (1975) 'The cardiac stress management program for Type A patients', *Cardiac Rehabilitation*, **5**, pp. 13–15.

SUINN, R.M. and BLOOM, L.J. (1978) 'Anxiety management training for pattern A behaviour', *Journal of Behavioral Medicine*, **1**, pp. 25–35.

SVENSSON, J. and THEORELL, T. (1983) 'Life events and elevated blood pressure in young men', *Journal of Psychosomatic Research*, **27**, pp. 445–56.

TAYLOR, S.E., LICHTMAN, R.R. and WOOD, J.V. (1984) 'Attributions, beliefs about control, and adjustment to breast cancer', *Journal of Personality and Social Psychology*, **46**, pp. 489–502.

THEORELL, T., DE FAIRE, U., SCHALLING, D., ADAMSON, U. and ASKEVOLD, F. (1979) 'Personality traits and psychophysiological reactions to a stressful interview in twins with varying degrees of coronary heart disease', *Journal of Psychosomatic Research*, **23**, pp. 89–99.

THEORELL, T., KNOX, S., SVENSSON, J. and WALLER, D. (1985) 'Blood pressure variations during a working day at age 28: Effects of different types of work and blood pressure level at age 18', *Journal of Human Stress*, **11**, pp. 36–41.

THOMAS, C.B. and DUSZYNSKI, K.R. (1974) 'Closeness to parents and the family constellation in a prospective study of five disease states: suicide, mental illness, malignant tumor, hypertension, and coronary heart disease', *Johns Hopkins Medical Journal*, **27**, pp. 372–5.

TOTMAN, R., KIFF, J., REED, S.E. and CRAIG, J.W. (1980) 'Predicting experimental colds in volunteers from different measures of life stress', *Journal of Psychosomatic Research*, **24**, pp. 155–63.

TROSTLE, J.A. (1988) 'Medical compliance as an ideology', *Social Science and Medicine*, **12**, pp. 1299–1308.

TURNER, J.R. and CARROLL, D. (1985a) 'Heart rate and oxygen consumption during mental arithmetic, a video game and graded exercise: Further evidence of metabolically-exaggerated cardiac adjustments?', *Psychophysiology*, **22**, pp. 261–7.

TURNER, J.R. and CARROLL, D. (1985b) 'The relationship between laboratory and "real world" heart rate reactivity: An exploratory study', in ORLEBEKE, J.F., MULDER, G. and VAN DOORNEN, L.J.P. (Eds) *Psychophysiology of Cardiovascular Control: Models, Methods, and Data*, New York, Plenum Press.

TURNER, J.R., CARROLL, D., SIMS, J., HEWITT, J.K. and KELLY, K.A. (1986) 'Temporal and inter-task consistency of heart rate reactivity during active psychological challenge: A twin study', *Physiology and Behavior*, **38**, pp. 641–4.

TURNER, J.R., CARROLL, D., COSTELLO, M. and SIMS, J. (1988) 'The effects of aerobic fitness on additional heart rates during active psychological challenge', *Journal of Psychophysiology*, **2**, pp. 91–7.

TYLER, P., CARROLL, D. and CUNNINGHAM, S.E. (1991) 'Stress and well-being in nurses: A comparison of the public and private sectors', *International Journal of Nursing Studies*, **28**, pp. 125–30.

VAN DOORNEN, L.J.P. (1986) 'Sex differences in physiological reactions to real life stress and their relationship to psychological variables', *Psychophysiology*, **23**, pp. 657–62.

WATERS, W.E. (1970) 'Community studies of the prevalence of headaches', *Headache*, **9**, pp. 178–86.

WATSON, C. and SCHULD, D. (1977) 'Psychosomatic factors in the etiology of neoplasmas', *Journal of Consulting and Clinical Psychology*, **45**, pp. 455–61.

WEINER, H., THALER, M., REISER, M.F. and MIRSKY, I.A. (1957) 'Etiology of duodenal ulcer: I. Relation to specific psychological characteristics to rate of gastric secretion (serum pepsinogen)', *Psychosomatic Medicine*, **19**, pp. 1–10.

WENGER, N.K. (1978) 'Early ambulation after myocardial infarction: Rationale, program components, and results', in WENGER, N.K. and HELLERSTEIN, H.K. (Eds) *Rehabilitation of the Coronary Patient*, New York, Wiley.

WENGER, N.K. (1979) 'Rehabilitation of the patient with acute myocardial infarction: Early ambulation and patient education', in POLLOCK, M.L. and SCHMIDT, D.H. (Eds) *Heart Disease and Rehabilitation*, Boston, Houghton Mifflin.

WICKRAMASEKERA, I. (1973) 'The application of verbal instructions and EMG feedback to the management of tension headache — Preliminary observations', *Headache*, **13**, pp. 74–6.

WILLIAMS, R.B., HANEY, T.L., LEE, K.L., KONG, Y., BLUMENTHAL, J.A. and WHALEN, R.E. (1980) 'Type A behavior, hostility, and coronary atherosclerosis', *Psychosomatic Medicine*, **42**, pp. 539–49.

WILLIAMS, R.B., BAREFOOT, J.C., HANEY, T.L., HARRELL, F.E., BLUMENTHAL, J.A., PRYOR, D.B. and PETERSON, B. (1988) 'Type A behavior and angiographically documented coronary atherosclerosis in a sample of 2,289 patients', *Psychosomatic Medicine*, **50**, pp. 139–52.

Note on the Author

Douglas Carroll is currently Professor of Psychology and Head of the Department of Psychology at Glasgow Polytechnic. He has researched and written widely on Health Psychology issues, in particular the role of psychological stress and behaviour in cardiovascular disease.

Index

'additional' cardiac activity, 23, 24–7, 30, 32, 68
adherence: factors relating to, 80–1
  factors unrelated to, 79–80
  improving, 84
  measurements of, 77–8
  to medication, 77
    levels of, 77
  varieties of non-, 78–9
adolescents: sexually active, and AIDS, 49–50
aerobic: exercise, 65, 68, 71, 72
    and blood pressure, 73–4
  fitness, and cardiovascular reactions, 67
    and psychological stressors, 69
Africa, sub-Saharan: AIDS in, 44–5
AIDS, Acquired Immune Deficiency Syndrome, vii, 43–53, 106
  and behaviour, 10, 46, 48–52
  campaigns, 49–50
  children born with, 44, 45
  incidence of, 44–5
  levels of knowledge, 50
  low personal risk belief, 51
  in Uganda, 82–3
alcohol: and immune system, 35
anaerobic exercise, 68
analgesic: hypnotic, 95–97
anger: and CHD, 18
  control of, 62–3
  suppression, and cancer, 40
angina pectoris, 12, 63, 89
  and socio-economic status, 104
antidotes, 2
antigens, 34
anxiety: and stress, 72
appraisal: denial, 6
  intellectualization, 6

ARC, AIDS-related complex, 43
aspirin: effectiveness of, 16
assertiveness: training in, 62
atherosclerosis, 12
  life style management programme, 63
  studies, 17, 18
Australia: AIDS campaign, 50
autoregulation theory, 23
AZT drug: for AIDS, 46

background stressors, 4
Baum, Andrew, 35
behaviour: and AIDS, 46
    reducing risks, 48–52
  and cancer, 39–40
  and disease, vii, 2, 9–10
  and medical compliance, 75
  and pain, 93, 96–7
  and socio-economic status, 105
  and stress, 9
  type A, vii, 7, 105
    categories, 13
    Consensus Report, 14
    and coronary heart disease, 11–21, 33
    and hypertension, 22–32, 55
    and life style, 20
    measurement of, 13–14
    pattern, 12
    as predictor of CHD, 15
    as risk factor, 61–3
    and serum cholesterol, 56
    and stress management, 57–8
    delayed, 62
    as trait, 20
  type B, vii
  varity of orientations, 17
  see also illness behaviour

bereavement: and immune system
efficiency, 38
biofeedback: and hypertension, 58–9
and pain, 93–5
biological make-up: and heart reaction to
psychological stress, 29
Black report (1980): and social
inequalities in health, 104–5
blood pressure: and exercise, 73–4
high, and hypertension, 22, 23
parental, 30
and race, 102, 103
and stress management, 59–61
womens', 99–100
BRS, Bortner Rating Scale, 13, 14, 15
Byrne, D.G., 20

caffeine: and immune system, 35
cancers, vii, 2
and behaviour, 10, 39–40
and depression, 38–9
and medication adherence, 79
and stress, 36–8
in animals, 37
in humans, 37–8
see also Kaposi's sarcoma
Cannon, Walter, 3, 24
cardiac reactions: to stress, 23–4, 27–9
see also 'additional' cardiac activity
cardiovascular disease, 2
see also heart disease
cataclysmic events, 3
CHD: *see* coronary heart disease
childbirth: and pain management, 95, 97
cholesterol: *see under* dietary cholesterol;
serum cholesterol
circumstantial non-adherence: to
medication, 79
cognitive restructuring, 54, 57, 62
competitiveness: and CHD, 18
compliance: in medication, 76–7
component analysis, 17–18
condoms: use of, and AIDS, 50, 51
contagious disease, vii
control: and occupational demand, 5
and pain, 88–9
and stress, 7
coping: active, 23, 28
and cancer, 41, 42
and exercise, 70, 72, 74
and life events, 39, 70
passive, 28
strategies, 6, 54
and race, 102

coronary heart disease (CHD): and
essential hypertension, 11
and gender mortality differences, 99
risk factors for, 11
in Sweden, 8
counselling: and HIV tests, 48
need for, with HIV, 53
non-compliance, 76
and stress management, 57
cultural values: and pain response, 87

daily hassles, 4, 5
and heart rate reactions, 28
death: causes of, vii, 2, 5
defence mechanisms, 6
de Geus, E.J.C.: and fitness tests, 68–9
depression, 1, 7
and cancer, 38–9, 40
and stress, 72
diathesis, 6
diet: for coronary atherosclerosis, 63
programmes, non-compliance, 76
and socio-economic status, 105
dietary cholesterol: and CHD, 55, 58
disease: lay theories of, 83
Dressler, William, 103

electric shocks: and pain studies, 88
emotional suppression: and cancer, 40
endorphins: and pain, 90
in placebo effects, 90–1
endurance exercise, 65, 67
environment, stressful: and cancer, 37
episodic analgesia, 87
essential hypertension: *see under*
hypertension
exercise: and blood pressure, 73–4
and coronary atherosclerosis, 63
moderate: for CHD, 65, 66
and well-being, 71
and physical fitness, 54
programmes, 8, 74
protective effect, of, 66–7
psychological benefits of, 70–3
and psychological stress, 67
see also aerobic exercise; anaerobic
exercise; endurance exercise;
leisure exercise

family resemblance: in heart rate
reactions, 29, 31
family support: and medication
adherence, 80, 81
fast speaking: and CHD, 18

feelings: and disease, 2
fitness: and psychological impact of stress, 70–3
'flight' or 'fight', 24
fluid retention: and psychological stress, 31–2
Framingham Heart Study, 14, 15, 22
French-Belgium Collaborative Heart Disease Study, 15
Friedman, M., 11, 57
FTAS, Framingham Type A Scale, 14, 15

gate control theory: and pain, 89–91
gender differences: and health, 98–101
gene systems: and fitness, 69
    and reactivity, 69
genetic predisposition, 6, 7
    and cancer, 42
germ model: of disease and illness, 2
Greer, Steven, 40

haemophiliacs: and HIV, 45
headache, 85
    tension, 86, 94, 95
health belief model: and AIDS, 51–2
    and medication adherence, 81
health communication: and medication adherence, 81–2
health psychology, vii, 1
    evolution of, 98
    and stress management training, 54
heart: and CHD, 11–12
    disease, vii
    rate, and oxygen consumption, 24–6
    reactions, 'real life', 28–9
    in families, 29
    and video games, 24, 27
heterosexual sexual transmission: of AIDS, 46
    and behaviour, 49–50
'hidden observer': in pain management, 95
high risk individuals: cardiac reactions to stress in, 29–31
    studies of, 16–17
HIV, human immunodeficiency virus, infection, 10, 43, 106
    incidence of, 44–5
    prenatal spread, 45, 46
    screening for, 46–8
        anonymous, 47
        continuous, 47
        voluntary, 47

symptoms of, 43
transmission of, 45–6
in Uganda, 82–3
Holmes, D.S.: review, 19–20
homosexuals: and AIDS, 43
    behavioural change, 49
hormones: in women, and CHD, 99, 100
hostility: and CHD, 18, 19
    and stress, 72
    and stress management, 62–3
hypertension: effect of exercise on blood pressure, 73–4
    established, 27
    family history, 31
    non-compliance, in medication, 76, 83
    programme, drop-out rate, 84
    and race, 102
    and reaction to stress, 22–32, 33
    as risk factor, 61–3
    and salt and fluid retention, 31–2
    and socio-economic status, 103
    and stress management, 58–61
hypnosis: and pain management, 95
    and placebos, 96
hypochondriasis, 9

illness: behaviour, and chronic pain, 9
    folk theories of, 82
    in women, 101
immune system: and HIV, 43
        and HIV test results, 48
    and stress, 33–42, 48
infectious diseases: elimination of, 2
IV, intravenous drug users: and AIDS, 44, 45, 47
    in Edinburgh, 52
    and heterosexuals, 46
    in Glasgow, 52

JAS, Jenkins Activity Survey, 13, 14, 15
    type A scale, 13
'John Henryism': and racial health differences, 102–3

Kaposi's sarcoma: and AIDS, 43, 44
kidneys: and blood pressure, 31–2
Kiecolt-Glaser, Janice, 34

laboratory stressors, acute, 8
Lazarus, Richard, 6
leisure exercise, 66
life expectancy: increase in average, 2
life stresses: and exercise, 65–74
life style: changes in, 65
        and medication adherence, 79

and disease, vii, 2
management, 63
race and health, 103
incongruity, 103
socio-economic status, and health, 105
womens', and CHD, 100
Lifestyle Heart Trial, 63
Light, K.C.: and physical fitness tests, 68
lymphocytes, 34
and HIV, 43

marital disruption: and immune system,
34–5
and physical illness, 35
material well-being: and stress, 63–4
medical compliance, 75–84
medication: and pain, 96
and stress management, 60
meditation: and stress management, 54,
55, 59, 62
men: bisexual, and AIDS, 45
health studies on, 98–9
illness of, compared to women, 101
mood: and exercise, 71
morphine: and pain, 90
mortality: and social class, 104
Moses, J.: fitness and well-being study, 71
MPQ, McGill Pain Questionnaire, 91–2
MRFIT, Multiple Risk Factor
Intervention Trial, 16, 18
Multicenter Postinfarction Research
Study Group, 16
mutagenic development: and stress, 36–7
myocardial infarction, 12, 23
recurrent, 16
and stress management, 56–8 *passim*

naloxone: and placebos, 90–1
needle exchange units: and AIDS, 52
negative life events, 3
New York, US: AIDS in, 45
Norris, R.: and psychological benefits of
exercise, 70–3, 75
Norwegian Army Parachute Training
School: heart rate study, 24
nursing: and occupational stress, 4–5

occupational stress, 4–5
occupations: low status, and CHD, 20
non-manual, and CHD, 19
opiate chemicals: natural, and pain, 90
see endorphins

pain: assessment, 91–3
measurement of, 91–3

behavioural expressions of, 92, 96–7
and injury, 85–7
perception, 86, 97
phantom limb, 86
psychological approach to
management, 85–97
tolerance, 87
pain, chronic: and illness behaviour, 9
management of, 54, 92, 97
parental blood pressure: and cardiac
activity, 30
Patel, C.H., 59–60
pathogens, 2
patients: forgetting therapeutic advice,
83–4
personality, and medication
non-adherence, 80, 84
pepsinogen: and ulcers, 6–7
personality, vii, 7
see also behaviour
personal stressors, 3
physical: exercise, 23, 54, 67
fitness, 8, 67
see also exercise programmes
physicians: estimates, of medication
adherence, 78
satisfaction with, 81
support of, 81
physiological homeostasis: and stress, 9
placebos: and pain treatment, 89, 97
and hypnosis, 96
pneumonia: and AIDS, 43, 44
Pooling Project Research Group, 1978, 58
positive life events: absence of, 4
positive orientations, 54
prescriptions: non-adherence to, 58
pressure diuresis, 31
psychological disposition: and cancer, 36
psychological influence: and pain, 91,
93–7
psychological stress, 3–5
and 'additional' cardiac activity, 23,
24–7
and behaviour, 9–10
and physical exercise, 67
and race, 102
in women, 99, 101
psychological stressors, 68
psychological support: for cancer
patients, 41
public health campaigns, 105

questionnaire assessment: for behaviour,
13

race: and health, 101–3
Recurrent Coronary Prevention Project, 57, 58
re-infarction: factors affecting, 16–17
relationship, loss of close: and immune system, 38
relaxation, and stress management, 54, 55, 57, 59, 62
  non-compliance, 76
  and pain, 93–5 *passim*, 97
risk: factor, and 'additional' cardiac activity, 25
  and exercise, 74
  and hypertension, 22
  and stress management, 61–3
of CHD, *see under* high risk individuals
Rosenman, R.H., 11

salt retention: and psychological stress, 31–2
San Francisco, US: AIDS in, 45
self-instruction: and stress management, 62
self-reporting: in medication adherence, 78
serum cholesterol: and CHD, 55–7
sexual behaviour, 10
  see also under AIDS
sexually transmitted diseases: reduction in, 51
side effects: of treatment, 81
SI, structured interview, 13–15
  passim, 17, 18
smoking: and socio-economic status, and health, 105
social class-mortality gradient, 105
social environment: and disease, 2
  and stress, 64
social support: as buffer against stress, 3, 7, 10
  and illness, viii
  and medication adherence, 80
  and women, and CHD, 100–1
socio-economic status: and hypertension, 104
  and mortality, 104
  race and health, 103
specificity theory: and pain, 85
step-test, 72
Steptoe, A.: and fitness studies, 68–9, 70
stress: effect on health, vii
  frequency of contact, 20
  and HIV, 48, 53

and immune function, 34–42
inoculation, 54
levels of, 8–9
and life events, 56
management techniques, 8
  and CHD, 54–64
  and multiple risk factors, 61
  and non-compliance, 76
  see also psychological stress
stressful events: impact of, 6
strokes, 23
Sweden: 18-year-olds in, and high blood pressure, 4
  and deaths from heart disease, 5
  and social support, 8
  unemployment, and immune system, 35–6
symptomatology: and medication, 83
  subjective, and stress, 9
  in women, 101

therapeutic prescription: adherence to, 75–84
Three Mile Island nuclear installation accident: and stress, 36
time management: training in, 62
treatment: side-effects of, 81
trigeminal neuralgia, 86
Turner, J.R.: and physical fitness tests, 67–8

Uganda: HIV infection in, 82–3
UK: AIDS campaign, 49–50
ulcers: and pepsinogen, 6
unemployment: and immune function, 35–6
university employees: and occupational stress, 4

vaccines, 2
video game studies: and heart rate and oxygen consumption, 24, 27, 28
  and physical fitness, 67
visual analogue scales: in pain assessment, 91
vulnerability: biological, 6–7, 8
  psychological, 7, 8

WCGS, Western Collaborative Group Study, 14, 15, 18
well-being: and exercise, 71

Western Electric Company, Chicago:
    depression and cancer, 39, 42
women: and AIDS, 44
    exclusive health concerns, 101
    health of, 98–101

    protective advantage, 99
Woodshop film, 6
work: social functions of, 35
work environment, 4
work stress: *see* occupational stress